Cultural China

文化
生活

Snapshots of a New China
Culture

Better Link Press

This book is edited and designed by the Editorial Committee of *Cultural China* series

Managing Editors: Xu Naiqing, Wang Youbu

Project Designers and Executive Editors: Wu Ying, Zhang Yicong

Editor: Patrick Wallace

Stories and photos provided by *Shanghai Daily*

Assistant Editor: Yang Xiaohe

Editorial Assistant: Li Mengyao

Interior and Cover Design: Yuan Yinchang, Li Jing

ISBN-13: 978-1-60220-401-0

ISBN-10: 1-60220-401-2

Address any comments about *Snapshots of a New China—Culture* to:

Better Link Press

99 Park Ave

New York, NY 10016

USA

or

Shanghai Press and Publishing Development Company

F 7 Donghu Road, Shanghai, China (200031)

Email: comments_betterlinkpress@hotmail.com

Computer typeset by Yuan Yinchang Design Studio, Shanghai

Printed in China by Shanghai Donnelley Printing Co. Ltd.

1   2   3   4   5   6   7   8   9   10

CONTENTS

CONTENTS

Preface

Many people define culture mostly in terms of tangible things. To them, culture is the architectural structures which grace our cities, the *objets d'art* found in dusty museums, and the ancient relics and artifacts strewn throughout archeological sites. Certainly, this is one aspect of a cultural heritage, and it is an aspect in which China is particularly rich. The Forbidden City, the Great Wall, the grottoes in Dunhuang, the Potala Palace, the Terra-Cotta Warriors ... one can go on and on about the many world-class places of cultural heritage that can be seen in China. In China there are some small villages full of quaint, little traditional houses and streets that look better than any postcard, however, most Chinese cities are modern, industrial, and constantly under construction. This is a place that is both lived in, and living and growing-it is not a museum. And, although the country has many tourist sites of great cultural interest, the country is not one, big tourist trap.

Another way of defining culture is in terms of intangibles. These intangibles can include the way people think and act; the way they celebrate and, just as importantly, *what* they celebrate; the crafts people employ in their daily lives, and the craftsmanship used to make them; and, finally, the many ways people entertain themselves and others. The focus of this definition is on the people, not things, though naturally people often use

things to express themselves and their personalities. When we talk about a craftsman, for example, being an intangible cultural heritage, we are not saying that his crafts are a cultural heritage, but that the knowledge and skills that he carries with him are a cultural heritage.

There are plenty of wonderful books about China that focus on tangible cultural artifacts, but this book-like the other books in the *Snapshot* series-tries to meet a desperate need by focusing more on people than things. With articles taken from the *Shanghai Daily*, this book covers everything from the Lantern Festival to Shaolin kung fu, and from stand-up comedy to traditional doll-making. Yes, some of the articles do talk about architecture, like the old Western-style residences of Shanghai, and some do mention *objets d'art*, like modern sculpture, but people make up the heart and soul of this book. We want to show how culture plays a part of and impacts the daily life of people in China, and to show a little of how Chinese people live, think, and see the world.

Everyone should visit some of the great places of cultural heritage in China sometime in their life. Yet, having done so, if they can also learn something more about the people of China, they will be much the richer.

Patrick Wallace

Chinese Festivals and Cultural Images

Red: The Color of China

Magazine editor Liu Xuewei bought a giant, paper fish to grace the pale wall of her Shanghai apartment. This stunning crimson fish does not match the snow-white tone of her apartment, but she wanted something red in the room since the Spring Festival, also known as the Chinese Lunar New Year Festival, is coming.

China's mania for red reaches its climax around the Spring Festival. In every shop, red merchandise springs up like mushrooms. This merchandise can range from the traditional good-luck couplets written on red paper, or as fashionable as lacy, red shorts.

The Chinese characters "恭喜發財" means "wishing you prosperity".

"年年 (every year) 有 (have) 余 (surplus)" expresses people's wish for a better life.

Every country leaves an impression of a unique color. For example, yellow Egypt, ocean blue Norway, or foggy, gray Britain. Bright, pure, heart-stirring red suits China the most. This is why a world-famous director like Zhang Yimou used red in such a lavish way in his award-winning movie, *Raise the Red Lantern*.

"Red is a thick, compelling color in my mind. If there's something red at home, such as a big red Chinese tie, the atmosphere will be different," says 35-year-old film producer Li Xiaojun. "But I cannot explain why red works on me that way. It's just a habit-a tradition that I'm so used to."

Zhong Fulan, a professor on folk custom from East China Normal University says this passion for red is a typical Chinese tradition.

"Red is the most festive color of all, as it symbolizes prosperity and flourishing," says Zhong. "Chinese believe red things can ward off evils and disasters, and thus bring them luck and joy."

A man furnishes a giant drum with a paper-cutting dog.

left: Workers hang red lanterns to add festivity to the Chinese New Year.

right: "Zhao Cai Mao" means money and treasures will be plentiful.

"In Chinese history there used to be an admiration for the color yellow, which is attributed to a respect for the earth by farmers," says Zhong. "But gradually yellow became the exclusive color for royal families."

Zhong notes that the Chinese's preference for red begun during the time of Huang Di[1]. Archeologists have found most fabrics in an unearthed mausoleum during the Warring States Period[2] are in different shades of red. The link with red to the New Year's celebration (and therefore the Spring Festival) originated in the legend of a monster called Nian. Ancient Chinese used the color red to frighten this monster away, preventing family members from being attacked. Of course, *nian* is also the Chinese word for 'year'.

Apart from using red to celebrate the Spring Festival, the Chinese also have the interesting habit of wearing red underwear during their zodiac animal year. Unlike the Western zodiac which is based on a cycle of twelve zodiac signs in one year, the Chinese zodiac has a different sign —always an animal—for each year. This cycle repeats itself every twelve years.

"I didn't wear red underwear during my last animal year, 11 years ago. That year I had bad luck, so I plan to strictly

Setting off Baozhu means a farewell to the previous year.

1 "The Yellow Emperor", who was the first sovereign of civilized China and recognized as the common ancestor of the Chinese people. Originally this title had spiritual and mythical connotations, but then later it was used to refer to emperors after they were deceased. The emperor Qin Shi Huangdi (259-210 BC), widely regarded as the founder of China, used "Huang Di" to refer to himself while he was still alive.
2 476-221 BC.

Those boat-shaped ingots symbolize wealth.

follow the rules throughout my animal year next year," says Li.

Red also plays an important part in Chinese wedding customs. Traditionally, brides dress completely in red. The couple is usually taken to the bridegroom's home in an old-fashioned, red sedan chair. Her wedding bed is covered with red quilts, while her dowry box is covered with red paper. If they get a son later, the couple will share in their happiness by sending eggs dyed red to their friends.

Not all Chinese people love red from their innermost hearts.

"I have a complicated feeling toward red," says Liu. "I have some red clothes, and friends always say I look good in red. But I seldom wear the clothes because red is too bold and stands out. I don't like the color, but I respect it."

"The Chinese have given too many meanings to this warm, exciting color," says 28-year-old architect Tao Le. "But I don't like this color, and feel Chinese red is a bit vulgar. I don't like colors embedded with meaning. However, red is sometimes necessary for some designs."

Red is by all means imbued with many meanings in China, from the past until today. There is always something red in the tender part of every Chinese person's heart.

(Story by Michelle Qiao, photos by Zhang Suoqing and Wang Rongjiang)

Bring on the
Lantern Festival

Ma Junqin's memory about the Lantern Festival, which falls on the 15th day of the Chinese lunar calendar, is always connected with a lantern made in the shape of rabbit.

"I used to live in a *shikumen* building[3] when I was a little girl. Every Lantern Festival, I was so impatient to wait to play with a rabbit lantern, made by my father," recalled Ma, a 23-year-old Shanghai student. "As soon as we had the dinner of *tangyuan*[4], I rushed out to join the parade of rabbit lanterns on the nearby street with my cousin. The street was full of kids pulling rabbit-shaped lanterns."

Originally, people hung lanterns in front of their doors to drive away evil spirits. However today, the lantern has become a symbol of the traditional Chinese culture, playing an important role in celebrations and ceremonies, especially during the Lantern Festival. The Chinese started celebrating the Lantern Festival in the Han Dynasty[5]. There are many different beliefs in the origin of the festival, but nearly everyone thinks the festival began as some kind of religious worship. The

3 *Shikumen* means "stone gate". It refers to the typical style of housing that Chinese people used in Shanghai in the late 19th and early 20th centuries. This style was distinguished by family residences connected with narrow alleyways, often leading to an inner courtyard. The alley leading out to the main street would have a small, stone gate as the entrance. While the arrangement of the houses and the gate would be typically Chinese in sensibility, the houses might often be more Western in outward appearance, many being made of red brick and several stories tall.
4 Stuffed balls of sticky-rice.
5 206 BC-24 AD.

Left: People enjoy the display of "Caideng", or colored lanterns in different shapes at Yuyuan Garden.

festival reached its peak during the Tang and Song Dynasties[6]. It featured various exotic lanterns made of paper, colorful glass and even jade. Folk tales were sometimes painted on them. During the Tang Dynasty, lantern displays would last three days during the festival. Though there was a curfew, the emperors would lift it during that time, allowing the people to enjoy the festive lanterns day and night. The largest Lantern Festival celebration, which continued for ten days, took place in the early 15th century. The emperor even had the downtown area of the capital, Beijing, set aside as a display center for the lanterns. Lanterns were sold there during the day, and lit and exhibited there in the evening.

Today, the display of lanterns is still the big event of the festival. Traditional lanterns always use bamboo strips or steel wire as the frame. A candle is put in the middle of the frame, and oiled paper, gauze or silk fabric covers the frame to create the flattering, soft glow. The lanterns are classified into two groups-toy lanterns and colored lanterns. Since colored lanterns are designed and produced for people to appreciate, they are large and delicate. On the other hand, paper toy lanterns, often made in animal shapes, were designed for children to play with. Rabbit-shaped lanterns had wheels, and were popular because they the easiest to make.

"When I was a little girl, rabbit-shaped lanterns were sold everywhere during the festival season. You could choose to buy one or make one yourself. Mine were always made by my father. They were bigger than the others," recalls Ma. "After dinner, kids from the neighborhood would hold a rabbit-lantern

A rabbit lantern made of plastic

6 The Tang Dynasty was 618-907 AD, and the Song, 960-1279 AD.

"Tangyuan" is the traditional food for the festival. Made of glutinous rice flour, it's sticky and round in shape, symbolizing family reunion and happiness.

parade. When we pulled our lanterns down the street together, it was like we were holding a great ceremony. The candlelight was so impressive, sparkling in the night. Children even held competitions to see whose lantern could go the fastest and whose candle could remain lit the longest."

Unfortunately, handmade toy lanterns are rarely seen in the market nowadays.

"I'm too old to play with a lantern, but I still want to find a paper one for my nephew to celebrate the festival with," says Ma. "But I cannot find one anywhere."

Though toy lanterns made of paper are now difficult to find, children can still enjoy modern lanterns made from plastic. As it is the Year of the Dog[7], lanterns are made in the shape of dogs this festival. "Paper lanterns are not as safe as the new types. They were easily burnt by the candle inside. Handmade ones have not been on the market for more than five years," says Qiu Ruixiang, a wholesaler who has been running his business at Chenghuang Temple for more than eight years.

Lantern Show

While people in Shanghai light firecrackers and eat *tangyuan* during the Lantern Festival, visiting the lantern exhibition at Yuyuan Gardens is another popular activity each year. This year's

7 2006.

To celebrate the Lantern Festival, there is a big Lantern show at Yuyuan, an ancient garden.

lantern show highlights the twelve Chinese zodiac signs, jokes, fun and a giant luck tree where visitors can tie cards containing their New Year's wishes. People can also go to a grand carnival, highlighting traditional Chinese folk art. In addition to learning calligraphy, paper-cutting, and Chinese opera, visitors can guess the answers to the 1,000 riddles written on lanterns.

Despite these festivities, people in China do not regard the Lantern Festival as important as before.

"But we still appreciate the significance of the festival," insists Gu Xiaoming, a professor of history at Fudan University. "People should always remember it's a time for rest, reunion and self-adjustment. People are under great pressure from work these days, and sometimes lack joy. The festival should remind us to be optimistic towards life and work," he says. After all, the festival is a good opportunity to get cheered up and gather together with family.

(Story by Ma Dan)

A Chinese-Style New Year

Decorating your home this Spring Festival will help you get into the festive spirit, can make your place look great, and might also change your luck when it comes to happiness, prosperity and good fortune this coming year.

After cleaning their houses both inside and out, Chinese people traditionally begin decorating their rooms to reflect an atmosphere of joy and festive fun. Some people plaster red banners around their doors. On these banners are Chinese characters which give a blessing of happiness, longevity, luck and prosperity for the New Year. Other people paste red paper-cuttings on gates, windows, walls and lamps in order to bring good luck to their families. Others fill their homes with flowers, fruit, and trays of sweets, as these are symbols of hope and prosperity. Naturally, since the Lantern Festival is only fifteen days after the New Year's, lanterns are popular decorations during the New Year's festival as well.

One of the most popular decorative articles for the Spring Festival are cloth tigers. Since the Chinese people regard the tiger as a symbol that wards off evil and protects wealth, cloth tigers are well loved. People also think these cloth tigers can help prevent illness and bring luck.

The materials used and procedures employed in making cloth tigers vary. Usually, a piece of cotton or silk is filled it with sawdust or course grain. Then

Red fire crackers are used as decorations, with real crackers lit to ward off bad spirits.

the silk is drawn on, embroidered, cut and patched to give the tiger a realistic shape and decorative pattern. These tigers are often made with enlarged heads, big eyes, big mouths and big tails to show their courage and power.

Smaller children also take great delight in wearing little tiger shoes. Tiger shoes are commonly found on babies' feet in rural China even today. The shoes are made entirely of cloth, and the toes are in the shape of a tiger's head. These beautiful, hand-sewn shoes are thought to carry within them magical wishes for protection. This is why Chinese parents make their children wear them. Fierce tiger faces, invoking the energy of the king of the beasts, were often used on children's clothing to frighten away evil, as well as to give the wearer the strength and courage of a tiger.

The cloth tiger hails from Shanxi Province

Paper Cuttings are traditionally used for decorations during the Chinese Lunar New Year.

These little shoes can also brighten your home, as they make a wonderful, whimsical wall or bookcase decoration.

Every Chinese household should also feature live, blossoming plants to symbolize rebirth and new growth. Flowers are believed to be symbolic of wealth and high positions in one's career. A home with a plant that blooms on New Year's Day is considered lucky, for the bloom foretells a year of prosperity. In the week before the New Year, special flower markets devoted to New Year blossoms open around the city.

In more elaborate flower arrangements, plum blossoms just starting to bloom are placed with bamboo and pine sprigs. The plum blossom signifies reliability and perseverance, while the pine evokes longevity and steadiness.

Left: Brightly colored tigers line the shelves at Esydragon on Taikang Road.

Right: A Chinese Lantern can add flair to your home.

Oranges and tangerines are also symbols for abundant happiness, so in warmer regions of China small orange or tangerine trees are common decorations or gifts during the Spring Festival. In colder areas, it is more common to see bowls of oranges or tangerines on the tables of most homes.

A bowl of oranges on the dining room table, a red scroll, a Chinese lantern-it does not have to be expensive, but adding just that little something can help you feel the hope and excitement of the coming New Year.

(Story by Yang Di)

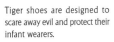

Tiger shoes are designed to scare away evil and protect their infant wearers.

Tea! A Key to China

Since many Westerners first learned about the Chinese culture from the tea ceremony, and an ongoing exhibition of tea sets at the Ji Gu Zhai Gallery is specially designed to show off Chinese tea culture and its thousands of years of history to foreigners and locals alike. The Ji Gu Zhai Gallery specializes mainly in Chinese ink-wash paintings and calligraphy, but on the second floor there is a private museum of 50 square meters, showcasing more than 120 ancient Chinese tea sets dating from the Spring and Autumn Period to the Qing Dynasty[8].

Long ago, Chinese people began to drink powdered tea. From picking to brewing, a cup of tea required a large variety of tools to make. These tools included pots, jars, mortars, pestles, trays, tripods, spoons, crushers and more. All of these tools are on display at the gallery.

Owner Yang Yuxin at his Ji Gu Zhai Gallery

Tea leaves had to be parched (i.e., dried) after they were picked. To do this, fresh tea leaves were placed on a parching tripod, and a fire was lit underneath. After the leaves were dried, they were powdered using a mortar and pestle. A parching tripod from the Warring States Period is on display, along with mortars and pestles made of stone from the Jin Dynasty[9].

8 The Spring and Autumn Period was 770-467 BC, while the Qing Dynasty was 1644-1911 AD.
9 The Warring States Period was 476-221 BC, and the Jin Dynasty, 265-420 AD.

This boat-shaped iron crusher held tea leaves, while a round stone with a hole in the center crushed them.

Of course, no afternoon or evening tea is complete without snacks. To hold these snacks, a five-mouthed bottle from the Jin Dynasty is on display. The mouths of the bottle were used to hold sesame seeds, peanuts, walnuts and pine nuts. Similarly, there is also a *ke*-a rectangular wooden plate divided into many sections. It was used to hold a variety of ingredients, including shallots, ginger, jujubes, and orange peel.

A boat-shaped, iron crusher, from the Ming Dynasty, may be the most eye-catching item on display. The boat-shaped body was used to hold tea leaves, while a round stone with a hole in the center, a *duo*, was used to crush them. Tea drinkers would put a stick through the hole in the *duo* and roll it back and forth in the crusher to powder the tea.

In making tea, the temperature of the water is a key factor. Stirring spoons were often made of copper or silver as both metals are good conductors of heat. When the water got too hot, the stirring spoon would be put in the water to absorb the heat, regulating the temperature. At the exhibit, a bronze stirring spoon from the Tang Dynasty is showcased.

This bronze stirring spoon from the Tang Dynasty was for regulating the temperature of the tea.

Sun Zhongwei and Yang Yuxin are the two men behind the museum- Sun is the main collector, and Yang is the owner of the Gallery.

Sun, 88, is a retired archeologist from the Shanghai Museum and a specialist in bronze ware. In his career at the museum, he saved some 100,000 pieces of bronze ware which might otherwise have been melted at the Shanghai Smelter.

In 1987, Sun was invited by eight of the biggest temples in Japan to take part in an academic exchange project. There, he was treated to the Japanese tea ceremony, a highly ritualized procedure different in many ways from the tea ceremony in China. While in Japan, one of his hosts noted that although tea originated in China, the tea culture has not been as well cultivated there. Spurred by this remark, Sun started to collect ancient tea sets so he could demonstrate the rich heritage of the Chinese tea culture.

Since 1987, he has been collecting tea sets from every antique market he can find. As an expert in antique tea utensils, whenever he goes to Fuyou Road, a street known for antiques, Sun is followed by a large crowd whose eyes fix on every article he touches.

茶壶

盐盒
战国

碾钵
晋
056

茶
宋

温碗
晋
032

茶瓶
宋
017

盏托
晋
075

碰
晋
009

Ji Gu Zhai Gallery displays more than 120 pieces of ancient tea sets.

Yang works at the Shanghai Gas Company. In 1993, the company opened a subsidiary, which is now the Ji Gu Zhai Gallery, and appointed Yang the manager.

Yang, 51, first met Sun in 1993. "I only knew him as an excellent painter," Yang recalls. "I didn't know he was an archeologist, let alone anything about his preoccupation with tea."

They then began exchanging ideas on painting. "But in 2000, a friend told me Mr Sun had a big collection of ancient tea sets," says Yang. "He wanted a stable place for their storage and display."

After discussion, Sun decided to donate his entire collection to Ji Gu Zhai. Yang and Sun made it a tea set museum.

"Sun told me he's happy to see everything going well in the past five years," says Yang. "He's very satisfied that his treasures are 'living' well in a right place."

Something about tea

●Tea was first recorded as a beverage in the Warring States Period (476-221BC). ●During the Tang Dynasty (618-907AD), tea culture expert Lu Yu wrote "The Theory of Tea" in 758 AD, the first book in the world introducing systematically how to grow, make and drink tea. ●Tea was used as food and medicine until the Tang Dynasty, when it became a popular beverage in China. During the exchange between China and the West, tea was brought abroad by Persian merchants through the Silk Road. ●During the Ming Dynasty (1368-1644), Zheng He's voyage brought tea to more countries in the world. ●To treat guests with tea has long been a practice and a custom for showing respect in China. A number of ancient Chinese poets such as Li Bai, Bai Juyi and Su Dongpo loved to depict tea in their works.

(Story by Zhou Tao, photos by Shen Kai)

This five-mouthed bottle from the Jin Dynasty was used to hold snacks.

Empress Eatery

In a small *hutong*[10] in Beijing's Houhai area, there is a dark courtyard with a restaurant that has only seven, plain tables. The restaurant does not have much of a signboard or even a menu to order from-you must eat the set course they provide. Yet, Family Li Imperial Cuisine is one of the capital city's best-known dining places.

Surprisingly, hundreds of global celebrities have wined, dined and lingered there. Crowds of bodyguards, policemen and luxurious cars are common. Famous guests include Bill Gates and the surviving imperial members of the Qing Dynasty, like Pu Jie, the brother of the last Qing emperor, Pu Yi. The food at the restaurant has been called "spectacular and unbelievable … a living history."

For four generations, the Li family guarded secret recipes smuggled out of the imperial kitchens by General Li Shunqing, who was once in

charge of the palace guards in the Forbidden City. He was responsible for the royal family's security. Since poisoning was always a threat, his duties included watching over the kitchen that prepared the food of the Empress Dowager Cixi

10 The *hutong* is the traditional kind of residential area in Beijing. It is typified by a narrow alleyway leading off of a main street to an inner courtyard. Most of the houses are low, one or two story affairs, with typical traditional Chinese sloped roofs. The houses and walls are often covered with plaster which has been painted dull-grey.

Sweet and Sour Ribs

(1835-1908). To escape detection, the general memorized the imperial recipes. After he resigned and returned to his hometown, he wrote down the menus, the ingredients, and the cooking processes used in the royal kitchen. This record was passed down from generation to generation.

"We cook the way people cooked years ago, without microwaves or pressure cookers. It's a time-honored method with contemporary ingredients," explains Li Shanlin, the general's grandson. Li, now in his eighties, was born into a royal family, remembering the glory of the last dynasty. He still remembers the luxurious life he lived when he was young: 30-plus servants, 90-plus rooms in his house. The garden contained all kinds of plants, spotted deer, peacocks, red-crowned cranes, and even its own artificial bridges and water fountains.

The little boy inherited all the aristocracy's lifestyle, the difference being that he not only enjoyed fine food, but also cooking it.

"I would spend a lot of time in the kitchen observing how the chefs fried meatballs, mixed the fillings with spices, controlled the temperature, and all the other crafts of cooking," Li recalls.

"Normally chefs would not teach their techniques to others. I usually went to the kitchen when they were busiest so they would ask me to assist them. In this way, I learned a wealth of cooking techniques over the years."

Li's father was one of those useless sons who possessed the finest things, but was poorly educated and irresponsible. Without mature management, the family fortunes gradually declined. The whole family moved from one place to another, from more than 90 rooms to a home with only a few rooms in the Yangfang Hutong in Houhai area, where the Li family live today. The fine living of childhood was replaced with poverty and misery.

Beijing Smoked Pork

Li remembers a long-ago experience: "During that time, we waited for a strong wind during the winter, because when the strong wind blew, the branches of the poplar trees would break and fall, so we didn't need to chop firewood."

Li lived in a small bungalow along with six family members. Since he was not physically strong, the whole family depended on his wife's small monthly income to survive in the mid-1960s. This kind of life lasted for about seven years.

"At that time my wife's salary was 69 yuan per month. However, the standard of living for even the poorest person was 12 yuan a month, and we didn't even meet the standard," he says. "I had to learn to ration food-especially since food coupons were needed to purchase meat-and practice my cooking skills."

Li learned to go fishing—which became his lifetime hobby—to get shrimp and fish to help with the food-shortage problem. He learned to use every part of his raw materials in cooking. For example, he would cook the lean meat, and then save the fat to produce oil for cooking vegetables, while the dregs of fat from the oil-refining process could be used to roll pastry.

According to Li, his complicated education background also helped a lot in his cooking. In 1939, he first entered the then Beijing Furen University and studied chemistry. After the establishment of the People's Republic of China, he studied Chinese architecture at Beijing University under famous architect, Liang Sicheng. Later, he taught himself mathematics and became a math professor in the Capital University of Economics and Business in

Well-stewed Superior Shark's Fin with Duck Meat

Beijing, until his retirement at the age of 71.

"Math skills have helped me to ration food well, and my architecture background taught me how to present the food in a way pleasing to the eye," Li notes.

Li has three daughters and one son, and they all inherited their father's love for food and cooking. In their spare time, the whole family cooked for themselves. The children prepared the materials and ingredients, while Li did the cooking. As the children grew up and their cooking skills improved, Li became the supervisor while the children were cooking, correcting their mistakes as strictly as when he taught mathematics in the university.

In 1984, China Central Television and *Chinese Food* magazine held a banquet contest to celebrate the 35th anniversary of the country's founding. The Li family was popular in their neighborhood, so they were encouraged to enter. Li's second daughter, Li Li, entered as one of more than 2,800 participants from all over the country. In a short two hours' time, Li Li prepared six cold dishes, eight hot dishes, one soup and a dessert. Her amazing skills easily beat the other contestants, and she won the championship.

Despite being the cooking contest champions, the family had never considered opening their own restaurant, since they had only three small rooms in a dark alley. Nevertheless, reporters kept visiting their house to interview them and they received scores of letters every day. All the neighbors encouraged them to open a restaurant.

Finally, Li began to plan. They had a family meeting and agreed to empty one room to open the restaurant. This was the beginning of the legend.

In May 1985, Family Li Imperial Cuisine opened in Beijing. At that time, the restaurant only set one table each day, and that table only accepted one reservation. The restaurant only serves set menus because each dish takes a long time to cook. For each dinner the family needs to work from the early morning until the clients come. Only in this way could they guarantee the quality.

"In our imperial cuisine, nutrition is the priority," Li stresses. "The dishes look simple. However, throughout the cooking process, all the raw materials must be strictly selected. All the dishes must be patiently cooked over a gentle fire."

In line with the different ingredients, various cooking methods are adopted. There are no modern cooking appliances in the kitchen, only the stove. All the cooking materials are natural. No artificial colors, flavors or additives are used. Usage of modern ingredients, such as tomatoes, is also forbidden, because "traditional Chinese dishes have nothing like a tomato, and the use of it would make the whole dish taste like Western food," Li says.

With the success of the Beijing restaurant, founder Li Shanlin finally decided to take his imperial cuisine to Shanghai. In cooperation with Visual Orient Ltd, which has brought to Shanghai wildly successful dining venues such as Sens & Bund and Bar Rouge, they have opened a new restaurant on the Bund.

According to Li, Shanghai, as a commercial metropolis, is known to have been influenced more by the Western culture rather than the traditional Chinese culture. "I want to introduce to Shanghai the authentic traditional Chinese culinary culture," the old man says.

Apart from Beijing and Shanghai, today Family Li Imperial Cuisine can also be found in Melbourne, Australia, and Tokyo, Japan, thanks to the efforts of Li's four children.

"We think it's meaningful to help my father to pass on the family cuisine, which has always been his lifetime mission," says Li Aiyin, the eldest daughter, who quit her job as a doctor to help her father run the business.

Recommended Dishes by Li Shanlin

●**Deep-fried Bean Cake (Chao Ma Doufu)** A traditional dish of old Beijing, *Ma* bean is a byproduct of making noodles from green beans. It looks like soybean curd. After being fried with ground meat and pepper oil, it tastes delicious and a little spicy. It stimulates the appetite and is good for the digestion. ●**Beijing Smoked Pork (Beijing Xun Rou)** It is made from the best pork, colored with natural vegetable juice without any artificial pigments, and then smoked for a long time. For presentation, it is simply cut into pieces and arranged on the plate. Different from regular smoked pork, the dish tastes sweet and sour without being fatty. ●**Well-stewed Superior Sharks Fin with Duck Meat (Ya Bao Yuchi)** The duck meat in the dish is Beijing duck, aromatized with natural flavors. The meat is boiled for some time before it is stewed with prepared shark's fin. The whole dish takes six to seven hours, and the taste of duck and shark's fin marry perfectly. ●**Deep-fried Fresh Scallops (Qing Song Xianbei)** The fresh scallops are imported from Australia and fried in a special way. It is served with a side dish of fried pickled kale. The two match perfectly in color, taste, aroma and presentation. **Fried Egg Custard (San Bu Nian)** It is a typical imperial dessert, favored by Empress Cixi. Though the name is simple, and there are only a few ingredients like yolk, sugar and water, it is difficult to cook. The ingredients must be mixed completely. It tastes soft and glutinous, but does not sticks to either the plate, chopsticks or teeth.

(Story by Michelle Zhang)

Chinese Traditional Arts

Fading Shadows

Though the curtain has come down on his three-day shadow puppet show, Pan Jingle's performance made a lasting impression on everyone who saw his artistry. Pan, with his tanned, wrinkled face, strong build and gnarled fingers, looks no different from any other weather-beaten farmer from western China's Shaanxi Province. However, when he is on stage, the 78-year-old really shines. He is one of the few remaining shadow puppet masters in Shaanxi, and is regarded as a "living fossil" of the old folk art.

Pan and his shadow puppet troupe present various ancient legends of China-love stories and folk tales acted

Shadow-puppet master Pan Jingle and his more-than-100-year-old *Yueqin*.

Shadow puppeteers from Huaxian Country in Shanxi Province during one of their performances during their three-day Shanghai tour.

out through the delicate movements of leather puppets. Every movement of the puppets is so lifelike that even real smoke is seen when a puppet character lights up a pipe.

Chinese shadow puppetry is widely considered to have originated in what today is Huaxian County, Shaanxi Province. The folk art has a long history going back more than 2,000 years, but took its present form during the Song Dynasty[11].

Born in the region that is the cradle of shadow puppetry, Pan has devoted more than 60 years of his life to preserving the ancient tradition which is in danger of becoming extinct. Constantly smoking a homemade pipe, Pan becomes excited when recalling his own shadow puppet debut:

11 960-1279 AD.

"It was on July 25, about 60 years ago," he says. He began to learn the art from a local shadow-puppet master, Liu Dewa, when he was 15. Although he studied under Liu for only one year, he was able to master all the skills needed and quickly became a local star.

"You could not be a successful shadow puppet artist without a lot of hard work," says Pan. "I practiced every day, even when it was snowing heavily outside." Although he has only a primary school education, Pan knows more than 200 shadow puppet plays by heart.

"The reaction of an audience is the only standard by which you can judge whether a puppeteer is good or not. That means you should not only act out the roles but also 'be' the roles you are playing, no matter whether they're male or female," he says.

Consulting history teachers in his hometown, doing research and studying the roles over and over again, Pan tries to master every role he plays. All the hard work and diligence has paid off, and Pan is now respected as an all-round shadow puppet master. This has enabled him to do a lot in his efforts to preserve the ancient performing art form.

Pan has long been famous for his silvery voice. His distinctive, resonant voice can be heard clearly throughout a theater without the aid of a microphone. He has to portray a wide variety of roles ranging from a formidable general to a mild-mannered young man, and from a naughty boy to a flirtatious lady.

To the accompaniment of simple musical instruments, his shows are in the typical Shaanxi Opera style. Since the shows have music, in addition to playing many of the roles in the puppet show, Pan also plays the *qiansheng*, a traditional, Chinese musical instrument.

Fading Shadows

"A shadow-puppet troupe is made up of five people-each plays about four to five ancient Chinese instruments like the two-stringed plucked *yueqin* and the bronze wind instrument, the *suona*," he explains.

The *qiansheng* player leads the puppet troupe in much the same way lead musician in a band leads the other band members. However, not only does he play the *qiansheng*, he also plays other instruments during the performances. All the old musical instruments enhance shadow puppet performances. Pan's *yueqin* is almost 100 years old. It has accompanied him since that July 25, some 60 years ago.

Shaanxi shadow puppet plays win audiences over through their lingering tunes, exquisite puppet designs, bright colors and the liveliness of the performances. However, today things are changing fast. As people have more choices in the ways they can find entertainment, shadow puppetry is facing oblivion. In Pan's hometown, few young people are interested in the old folk art-his youngest student is already 49 years old.

"If things go like this, I will bet that shadow-puppet plays will soon die out," Pan says sadly. "The biggest problem facing the preservation of shadow puppet is a lack of funds."

Pan's youngest son, Pan Liang, is good at creating shadow puppets but he lacks a good voice. However, much to his delight, the senior Pan's youngest grandson seems to have fallen in love with the art form.

"But I don't want him to learn more about it just now, because he has to go to school first," Pan says.

(Story by Ma Dan, photos by Li Qingtian)

Identity Preservation

The ancient Yunnan Plateau, one of the early breadbaskets of mankind, nurtured China's early primitive cultures. In this southwestern province, there are 25 distinctive minorities with hundreds of sub-branches, each with its own lifestyle, history, custom, culture and art. Due to geographical barriers, like mountains and raging rivers, the changing forces of time lose their intensity when it comes to Yunnan. Many ancient rituals, chants and dances have been remarkably preserved there, glimmering with the brilliance of ancient cultures.

The Yunnan Yuansheng Music and Dance Studio, under the leadership of Liu Xiaojin, has undertaken the role of preserving the diminishing ethnic dances. The studio is comprised of indigenous Yi and Wa minority artists from remote villages throughout the province. From keening songs, earthly yells and charming lovely duets, to ritual dances of family, agricultural and spiritual life, their artistic performances are surprising, immediate and profoundly moving.

A minority musician plays an instrument.

The dances have a visceral power.

Minority musicians from Southwest China's Yunnan Province perform their ethnic art.

Liu, a filmmaker, spent seven years documenting the late composer Tian Feng and his Yunnan Ethnic Culture Preservation Institute. Now she herself works to preserve and document the indigenous cultural traditions of the villages where the artists live and work.

"They are all farmers in real life," says Liu. "Their performances are rooted in their daily life, without any artificial polish or professional background. They have accumulated over thousands of years their ethnic culture, especially their sacrificial rites. Through generations, they have retained the most classical elements," she adds.

Commenting about the ethnic make-up of the performers, she remarks, "Even in the 1950s, Wa people still had the tradition of cutting men's heads off and offering them to the ancestors. From this, you can see that it was a quite isolated society."

Yan Bing is a 60-year-old artist of the Wa minority, whose father,

Yan Bing, a 60-year-old artist of Wa minority, plays a traditional instrument. Yan is known as the "king of Wa music".

according to Liu, is head of a Wa tribe in Ximeng County. His love for music emerged at an early age. Because of his family, he was able to absorb the traditional songs, rhythms and instrument-making skills of the Wa. Yan worked for the Ximeng County Culture Department for more than 30 years, specializing in collecting and cataloguing Wa music and instruments. He is the most famous Wa artisan in Ximeng, where he is known as the "King of Wa Music."

Liu says Yan can play more than 40 different instruments, all made by himself. "Few people are able to make those local instruments," Liu notes.

Yan was invited by the late composer Tian in 1997 to give lectures about the Wa people at the Yunnan Ethnic Culture Preservation Institute. There, Tian had recruited both teenaged students and elder artists from different tribes to teach them.

Hou Baoyun was another artisan teacher at the Institute, teaching the songs and dances of the Yi minority. A versatile and locally famous musician, he has been recognized as a "Master Folk Artist of Yunnan" by the Yunnan Government. Hou says the ethnic culture is dwindling as the young people in his village only like pop music and modern dance. "In the past, most people could dance and sing. When I was young, I sought out four teachers to teach me folk music and dance," says Hou.

Now with the support of Liu's Studio, Hou has started to teach young people in his own village again. "The class started last November with 50 students. I work in the farm during the day and teach them at night," he says.

Last year, with the help of China Yunnan International Culture Exchange Center and Liu, twenty artists from the Studio were invited to perform in the John F. Kennedy Center for the Performing Arts in the United States. The show was an immediate success.

"It was such a pleasure to play in the US. The seats were full and even the passageway were packed," Hou recalls.

"They all thought it was great performance. When minority artists were performing on stage, the audience was so quiet sitting and watching. But when they stopped, they applauded for a long time," says Liu, who led the 2005 American tour.

However, the biggest concern for Liu's studio is

Minority musicians dancing.

funding. After all, a lack of money caused of the collapse of Tian's Institute. "A Hong Kong gallery has donated 110,000 yuan, which covers the rental and the teachers' payment," say Liu. "But we still need more money."

Delighted by the positive response from the audience during the Studio's debut in Shanghai, Liu is now planning to cooperate with Shanghai's universities. Performing for students is her first step to get more people know about the Yunnan indigenous dance and music.

"I didn't realize the significance of folk performing art in the beginning, but after I learned about it, I began to think if we don't care for it, it may totally disappear within a decade. That would be horrible," says Luo Fengxue, 30, who has been learning *wushiji*, a Yunnan folk drum, for four years.

Chen Qiaoqiao says she is amazed by the Studio's primitive yet original performances. "I think the indigenous people are above all others in the world. They have a huge power, deeply rooted in the land. People should pay more attention to nature, otherwise modern society will totally destroy it sooner or later," says Chen.

Ethnic academy

●The Yunnan Ethnic Culture Preservation Institute was founded by Tian Feng, a well-known Chinese composer and professor of Beijing-based Central Conservatory of Music in 1993. ●Tian became fascinated with the local music since after his first visit to Yunnan in the 1980s. ●The institute, situated in the town of Anning outside of Kunming, was established in the hope of preserving and teaching the cultural traditions of Yunnan's ethnic groups. ●After Tian's death in 2001, businessman He Jinxin tried to sustain the institute, but by the end of 2002 it closed.

(Story by Wu Yingying, photos by Shen Kai)

Stand-up Comedy
Makes a Comeback

Known as "grassroots artists" (artists who were born humbly, but with special talent in art), Shanghai stand-up comedian Cai Ruhua and Beijing-based *xiangsheng*[12] performer Guo Degang are in the spotlight this year, drawing a young generation into these traditional art forms.

Cai, a 44-year-old Shanghai native, has been featured frequently and recently in newspapers, websites and on TV because of his stand-up comedy. He has been making audiences laugh with his original jokes on the latest hot topics for one-and-a-half hours each night since 1997 in the tea house on Haining Road.

12 A kind of stand-up comedy from north China.

Shanghai stand-up comedian Cai Ruhua performs on stage at a local tea house.

In one of his jokes, a little girl says to her father, "Dad, I hear something called 'bird flu' kills chickens and ducklings. I think those who walk on two legs are all in danger. You walk with two legs too, so you'd better crawl, not walk."

"On an average, people laugh 96 times and applaud 36 times during my one-and-a-half-hour performance every day," says Cai, who keeps count.

During his nine years of performances, the tea-house has expanded in capacity from 50 seats to 300 seats to accommodate a growing

STAND-UP COMEDY

Beijing based *xiangsheng* comic Guo Degang

audience. Tickets sell so well that now people have to book a 20-yuan ticket weeks in advance, and even then it is still very difficult to get one.

"This is my first time here," says Song Yuehua, a middle-aged man visiting the tea house with a couple of colleagues. "I read about him online and booked tickets 10 days ago."

"I know Cai very well, as I've been coming to his shows since the mid-1990s when he performed in a ballroom," says Zhang Jianhong, a middle-aged woman who reserved a big table for her friends in the first row at a recent show. "It's a good place for a get-together with friends. We can afford it. Cai's jokes have a conventional wisdom in them-he says in his jokes that it's bad to play mah-jongg, so we don't play it anymore."

Maybe Cai owes something to his counterpart, Guo Degang. The Tianjin native, now based in Beijing, became an instant hit due to an Internet craze for stand-up online comedy last year.

There is also a parallel with *Super Girl* (a Chinese version of *American Idol*). While some music lovers were arguing who should be China's Super Girl, *xiangsheng* lovers were listening to Guo's performances in tea houses in the capital. They have also been putting some of his performances online. The soaring level of downloads drew media attention, finally making Guo a household name in much of the country.

Of course, while Guo is popular in the rest of China, people in Shanghai, who are not big fans of *xiangsheng*, still prefer their own homegrown brand of humor.

Like Andy Kaufman, Cai, better-known by his nickname "Galiang"[13] started his career in the 1980s as a pub singer, imitating pop stars.

"I became a laborer after my graduation from high school," recalls Cai. "Manual labor was tough and dull. One day, I saw a beggar playing the guitar on the street, and I started learning the guitar from him. Later, I sang songs in pubs."

In 1989, Cai went to Shenzhen, Guangdong Province, where he saw Hong Kong-style TV talk shows, which inspired him to create his own performance style that features jokes, singing and improvised audience interaction.

Cai came back to Shanghai in 1991 with his own routine as well as his trademark appearance and costume-a hairstyle, shirts, and suits from the late 1980s and early 1990s Hong Kong. That look is still part of his signature performance now.

"My performance is neither *xiangsheng* nor singing," says Cai. "It's a one-of-a-kind."

Cai first performed in pubs, and then signed a 10-year contract with the tea house in 1997. "I saw Cai performing in other pubs, singing and telling jokes," says Sun Lanhua, owner of the tea house. "I thought it would be a good idea to hire him."

The most amusing but most difficult part of stand-up comedy is improvisation. Cai is skilled in it and well-experienced in interacting with audiences. Sometimes, however, he gets into trouble.

13 In the Jiangsu dialect this refers to a man wearing glasses.

Audience members burst into laughters upon hearing Cai's improvised Jokes.

"Although I can make people laugh with a few words,' says Cai, "some jokes really bugged people and involved naughty language. But I'm working hard to improve."

In China, most stand-up comedians belong to state-run troupes, and give shows in theaters or play in sitcoms. The lack of competition, practice, interaction with audiences and inability to improvise are major reasons the art form is gradually dying out. On the other hand, grassroots artists like Cai and Guo have to earn a living with every single joke. For this reason, their jokes must be attractive, fresh, and above all, funny. "I'm forced to develop my ability," says Cai. "You must make people willing to pay to listen."

With intensive practice and rich experience in live performance, grassroots artists know what audiences really want better than formal performing artists do. Their experience contributes greatly to their rise in popularity today, after years in which their fame only spread by word of mouth.

Cai's singing and joke-telling is relaxing. His recipe is to "think of audience members as cousins ... I have a glib tongue to give glib answers in any situation," says Cai. "But, if I moved to grand theaters-and that's what many people are suggesting to me now-the physical distance would prevent me and the audience from talking to each other. It would be very bad. What's worse, if the art becomes very popular and then becomes high art in grand theaters, where and how can common people find amusement?"

Although Cai and Guo share something in common-neither has a formal artistic education and theirs is considered low art-there is little comparison between them, except that they are the symbols of grassroots in Shanghai and Beijing.

"Funny plays" north and south

●Xiangsheng ●●*Xiangsheng* originated in Beijing and Tianjin in the late 19th century. If there is one comedian, it's called *dankou*. If there is a pair of comedians, it's called *duikou*. ●●The one on the left is called *The dougen* and the one on right is *The penggen*. Usually *The dougen* talks far more than *The penggen*. If there are three or more, it's called *qunkou*, but it's very rare. ●●The comedians tell jokes or stories satirizing various topics. The art was popular from the late 1970s to late 1980s in China. However, with the spread of television, the *funny men comes* increasingly gave shows in TV studios, instead of live performance on stage. The shows are shorter because of the rapid pace of TV. ●Huajixi ●●A similar situation exists in South China. Shanghai has its own farce (*huajixi* in Mandarin) performed in The Shanghai dialect. ●●It originated in the 1910s and was a combination of vendor' hawking wares, operas from Jiangsu Province and Western drama. It might have one actor doing stand-up comedy or might be a long play with many characters. ●●It recorded that the very first performer of Shanghai farce was Wang Wuneng (1892-1933), once a dramatic actor. In 1912, he tried a monologue in his show, involving jokes, singing and imitating dialects. It was very successful and considered the very first Shanghai comic routine. ●●Though it boomed from the late 1970s to early 1990s, its popularity has declined today.

(Story by Zhou Tao)

Yu Ji, the Beauty

In 1922, the Beijing Opera classic, *Farewell My Concubine*, premiered in Beijing. The play revolves around Yu Ji, a beloved concubine of the historical figure Xiang Yu[14].

In the play, Yu spoke of Xiang:

My Lord is stubborn by nature. Never does he accept sincere advice. What I fear is that the Great Conqueror of Chu could lose, betraying his decades-long fame as an undefeated hero.

14 Xiang (232-202 BC), overthrew the Qin Dynasty (221-206 BC), but later committed suicide after being defeated by Liu Bang (256-195 BC), founder of the Western Han Dynasty (206 BC-24 AD).

These lines form the heart of the play. They have recently been developed into a brand-new Yueju Opera story Yu Ji, the Beauty, which debuted in Shanghai as part of the celebration of the 100th anniversary of the birth of Yueju Opera.

Originating in Zhejiang Province, with only narration and singing but no accompaniment, the Yueju Opera is now one of the most popular Chinese traditional theaters in the region south of the Yangtze River. Since nearly all of its performers are female, the Yueju Opera is excellent at expressing emotions in a delicate manner. The songs are pure, sweet and agreeable, containing rich regional folk flavors. The performances are vivid and tender.

Classical Yueju Opera plays include love stories, such as *A Dream of Red Mansions*, written by Cao Xueqin, arguably China's greatest literary

masterpiece, and *West Chamber Romance*. However, *Farewell My Concubine*, set against the epic war between Liu Bang and Xiang Yu, was never considered suitable for the Yueju Opera, and this is the first time for the story of Yu and Xiang to be adapted to this art form.

In the story, Yu Ji, the beloved concubine of the general Xiang Yu, has an adopted brother, Zhang Liang. He later became a counselor of Liu Bang, who was Xiang's rival. Zhang is captured by Xiang, but saved at a crucial moment by Yu, who suddenly recognizes him. Four years later, Xiang is besieged by Liu's army in the city of Gai Xia. Unwilling to see Yu die with him, Xiang pretends to be drunk and drives her away. Yu leaves and encounters Zhang, who has come to take her out of danger. However, she declines his offer and returns to Xiang. The couple says their last farewell. Then Yu commits suicide, leaving the hope of living to her husband.

"It's a courageous adventure for us, since generally Yueju is not accomplished in reflecting big historic events like this one-Liu and Xiang fought to reign the country," says Shan Yangping, who played Yu. "We try

to interweave into the heroic tragedy of Xiang a beautiful, sad love story."

"Through Yu's eyes, we see the war and her heart. We feel its bitterness," Shan says. "We've made bold innovations. My Yu Ji is different from most other Yueju Opera heroines who are weak and vulnerable. She is graceful and highly spirited."

To achieve this, she has been training herself to sing more powerfully and make bigger gestures

on stage. "To walk away from my regular style isn't that easy. Yu Ji exhausts me. The only comfort is that I eat a lot but still lose weight," she jokes.

Instead of using a male performer as Xiang, *Yu Ji, the Beauty* uses a female to play this ultimate in masculinity.

"I'm the first *xiao sheng*[15] specialist to play Xiang in traditional theater," says Wu Fenghua, vice director of Zhejiang's Shaoxing Little Hundred Flower Yueju Opera Troupe. "To display this conqueror's formidable strength and personality, I borrow the performing skills from the *lao sheng*[16] profession in Yueju and even *hua lian*[17] from Beijing Opera."

In this opera, the simple storyline is made more complicated. Relations between different characters are more complex, and the love between

15 Young male.
16 Old male.
17 Forceful character with a painted-face.

husband and wife — along with brother and sister — as well as their many conflicts are illustrated through careful storytelling.

"The play in the Beijing Opera focuses on displaying the performer's personal artistic skill and charm, whereas in Yueju, it attracts the audience through enriched plots and upgraded set," says Wu Ying, vice director of China Mei Lanfang Cultural and Artistic Research Center. "I watched the rehearsal and found interesting elements from modern lives."

In one scene, Yu and Xiang drink from big jars filled with white wine, exchanging a final farewell. "Ancient Chinese beauties drank from small cups only, so this is really bold and imaginative," Wu says with a smile.

He says that the adaptation represents a big breakthrough for Yueju. "More significant is that we've seen through this attempt a better way of marketing our traditional culture-Yueju borrows the stories and skills of Beijing Opera so that it may also seize the Beijing Opera lovers' heart, and vice versa," he says.

(Story by Fan Meijing, photos by Wang Rongjiang)

Role Reversal

Hu Wenge walked gracefully onto the stage, bowed slightly to the audience and began singing. His character was Cheng Xue'e, a beautiful young woman in the Ming Dynasty[18], the heroine of the famous Beijing Opera, *The Phoenix Returns to the Nest*, written by the most outstanding proponent of the Beijing Opera, Mei Lanfang (1894-1961).

Though dressed in a dark brown suit without any stylized facial make-up, Hu was faithful to the role. His voice, accompanied by a small orchestra consisting of drums, *erhu*, *huqin* and *yueqin*[19], was artificially high-pitched, very charming and totally feminine.

Ripples of applause were given to Hu, the biggest star of this "Peking Opera Qiandan and Kunsheng" concert held at Shanghai's Yifu Theater. *Qiandan* refers to a male playing a female role, and *kunsheng* refers to a female playing a male role. Altogether twelve *qiandan* and *kunsheng* players performed, and the theater was fully packed.

"*Qiandan*, the most splendid and traditional element of the Beijing Opera, had disappeared for decades. Currently the number of *qiandan* actors is very limited,"

Wang Peiyu applies make-up to her face before a show.

18 1368-1644 AD.
19 The *erhu* and *huqin* are kinds of fiddles, while the *yueqin* is a kind of mandolin.

says Hu, who is one of ten students of Mei Baojiu-son of Mei Lanfang-and the only male learning to perform female roles.

"I'm lucky since I have many chances to perform on stage," he sighs, "but most other *qiandan* actors are simply trudging on a dim and rough career path."

Due to long-time prejudice rooted in the minds of the general public and professional performers themselves, *qiandan* and *kunsheng* are regarded as a "forbidden zone" in the Beijing Opera art.

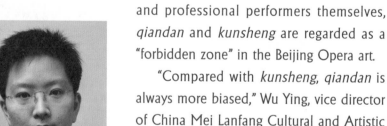

Kunsheng singer Wang Peiyu.

"Compared with *kunsheng, qiandan* is always more biased," Wu Ying, vice director of China Mei Lanfang Cultural and Artistic Research Center. "Actors like Hu are viewed as alien, and their numbers are no more than those endangered animal species."

Though mistreated nowadays, *qiandan* was once the only way of playing female roles in Beijing Opera. Only men were allowed on stage when this performing art was first invented more than 150 years ago, and women were totally excluded from the theater, even as spectators.

It was not until about half a century ago that the ban was lifted and women began to appear on stage. Later, troupes consisting of all female members were formed and actresses specializing in impersonating male roles took to the stage. Gradually, social consensus was reached that males should perform as males and vice versa. As a result, *qiandan* and *kunsheng* became out-moded.

However, the former splendor of *qiandan* and the great contribution *qiandan* singers made to Beijing Opera can not be denied. The four most outstanding performers of female roles in Beijing Opera history-Mei Lanfang, Cheng Yanqiu (1904-1958), Shang Xiaoyun (1900-1976) and Xun Huisheng (1900-1968)-are all men. Mei, besides his significant

Wu Wenge ties his hair up in front of a mirror before a performance.

personal artistic accomplishment and enormous efforts in educating young performers, was also the first artist to introduce the age-old quintessential art of China to an overseas audience, helping it to earn international recognition.

The question is why, now that woman can perform woman, are *qiandan* still needed? Hu gives his answer: "Theater is an art involving much exaggeration. It's beyond true life and should be viewed from a distance. To keep *qiandan* alive really is a process of maintaining tradition."

Hu used to be a pop singer, but quit in 2000 to throw himself into the Beijing Opera's art. Previously, he earned 50,000 yuan for singing at one pop concert. Now, his monthly salary is only about 1,000 yuan. The decision was hard to make but Hu does not regret it. "I have loved the Beijing Opera since I was a little boy. To me, it's divine," he says, full of emotion. "Master Mei's arts and skills are always enchanting. They are so complex that I will be learning until my last day. Money is trivial. My only consideration is how to perform better."

Wang Peiyu, a *kunsheng* actress at Shanghai Beijing Opera House, and one of the best of the younger singers, says excellence of performance is the strongest argument for settling disputes.

"The point is not that the role should be played by a man or woman, but that it be vivid and attractive," she says.

A love of the art is the only explanation for these actors and actresses' devotion to the Beijing Opera. They have been accustomed to fighting for a brighter future all alone, but still, their hearts are yelling for more public support.

"We hope people will become more aware that *qiandan* is a great artistic form that should be esteemed and passed down to future generations," Wu says, expressing his biggest wish.

However, when being asked if they are confident in the revival of *qiandan*, both Wu and Hu force a bitter smile and choose to keep silent.

The traditions and conventions

● The modern Beijing Opera first came into being about 150 years ago during the Qing Dynasty (1644-1911) by combining and integrating various opera styles such as Kunqu and Qingqiang operas. ●The various roles in The Beijing Opera are divided into four categories: *Sheng* (leading male characters), *dan* (females), *jing* (males with painted face), and *chou* (clowms). ●The major elements are *chang* (singing), *nian* (dialogue), *zuo* (pantomime), *da* (acrobatic) and *wu* (dancing). ●The repertoire of Beijing Opera mainly originates from tales from previous ages, important historical events and legends about famous figures. Most plots and characters' every gesture and movement are highly stylized and rest on long-standing conventions.

(Story by Fan Meijing, photos by Wang Rongjiang)

Costumes swirl as members of the Cloud Gate Dance Theater perform their dance version of the Chinese story *A Dream of Red Mansions*.

"Dream" Dances to an End

The final curtain came down last weekend on the stunningly beautiful Cloud Gate Dance Theater production of *A Dream of Red Mansions*, but the performance will stay in the memories of the Shanghai audience forever. The two performances in the Shanghai Grand Theater last week were the final ones for a production which has been performed around the world since it was launched in 1983. Lin Hwai-min, the founder of the Cloud Gate Dance Theater, made the decision to close down the show. The fabulous, embroidered costumes for *A Dream of Red Mansions*, designed according to Beijing and Kunqu Opera costumes, will now be put on display in museums.

"Cloud Gate and I have outgrown this production, which has 10,000 details and is so tiring," says Lin. "The farewell to the dance reminds me of a Chinese poem about lotus leaves, which says that life is all about the joy of birth, and the sorrow of passing away."

The dance drama was inspired by one of the four great classic novels of ancient China, and follows the lives of the members of several large and wealthy families. Lin, who was described as "Asia's Hero" in Time Asia Magazine this year, says that people unfamiliar with the original work would still be able to understand the dance version.

"Dance may not be good at telling a narrative, but it is good at creating an atmosphere," says Lin. "I have tried to show the youth and death of a young girl, and through the metaphor of the four seasons, the life and death of a family.

"Personally, I love this dance version of *A Dream of Red Mansions* a lot because I like seeing so many colorful beauties," says Lin. "And the set is very beautiful, like an oil painting. However, this grand production requires at least 25 dancers, and the regular Cloud Gate troupe numbers just over a dozen. I have to recruit new dancers. It's very hard to control the quality and balance between veteran dancers and newcomers."

"It's a hard job to be a Cloud Gate dancer," says Ching-chon Lee, who has been a dancer in the theater since 1983, when she was only 17. Lee danced the role of the girl in red in *A Dream of Red Mansions*.

"The dancers have to practice eight hours a day, learn Chinese boxing, tai chi, meditation, Chinese opera movements, ballet and contemporary dance. If it sounds very complicated it is because the dancers have to master every school but still be able to mix them together naturally," she says.

When asked about his immediate plans, an exhausted Lin replies, "The only thing I want to do right now is to go home and sleep, or maybe go and live in a desert in Africa. I don't want to write any more. I want to read a lot of books, watch DVDs and listen to music.

"Now, all I want to do is live without having any responsibilities for a while."

Born in Taiwan in 1947, the gray-haired, bespectacled Lin started writing novels at the age of 14. He had his first book published at 22. After attending an international writers' workshop at the University of

Cast Members of the Cloud Gate Dance Theatre with founder Lin Hwai-min (left) - who is also the creator of the dance version *A Dream of Red Mansions.*

Iowa in the United States, Lin sought out modern dance icon Martha Graham in New York, and became a student at her school. Later he studied the classical court dances of Japan and South Korea. Returning home, he established the Cloud Gate Dance Theater in 1973, the first contemporary dance company in Taiwan.

Cloud Gate is the name of the oldest known ritual dance in China, which dates back to around 3,000 BC. Lin bases Cloud Gate's repertoire on Asian myths, folklore, and aesthetics, but has given these ancient tales and artistic sensibilities a distinctively contemporary twist.

"I think Lin has brilliantly fused dance techniques and theatrical concepts from East and West, and that's why Cloud Gate has remained so successful and so popular," says local music critic Wang Shu, a big

Cloud Gate fan who has a VCD collection of all Cloud Gate's dance productions.

The Cloud Gate Dance Theater has enjoyed high acclaim at home in Taiwan since its foundation. The theater performs regularly in venues ranging from the prestigious theaters in Taipei to high-school auditoriums in remote villages. Free outdoor performances draw audiences of 30,000 people even on rainy days, and up to 80,000 when the weather is fine. Cloud Gate had also made many overseas tours.

"At my age," Lin says, "I still have two or three mountains to climb. I cannot always be looking back-I have to move on. I'm only interested in potential and possibilities. If I'm clear of everything, I won't do a job. The fun is all about adventure. I like vague or seemingly. I don't want to be disturbed by ghosts from 20 years ago."

Sometimes artists have to say good-bye to past glories to create something new. This beautiful version of *A Dream of Red Mansions* is gone from the stage forever, but surely there is more than just a "vague potential" of more dream-like creations coming from Cloud Gate. Recently, Lin began concentrating on a new dance entitled *Cursive III*, the final installment of his Calligraphy Trilogy.

(Story by Michelle Qiao, photos by Wang Rongjiang)

Traditionally Innovative

Taiwanese artist Wu Hsing Kuo is probably the most popular character currently in Shanghai's dramatic art scene. In 2006, he and his Contemporary Legend Theater (CLT) staged a thrilling adaptation of the 1969 Nobel laureate Samuel Beckett's signature piece *Waiting for Godot.* Wu and another three actors "China-ized" the Western play by presenting it through the language and style of traditional Peking Opera.

"CLT's *Waiting for Godot* is the least-boring *Waiting for Godot* I have ever seen," says Pan Yu, a drama fan who watched the play. "The actors have given the Western classic a new life. Such a fusion is quite impressive and also helps the Beijing Opera reach a bigger audience."

Hide - Kunju Opera (Ke Jun)

Later that year, Wu took another innovative approach with *King Lear*, adapted from William Shakespeare's dark play, which was staged in Shanghai as part of the local drama arts center's joint program with the House of World Cultures in Germany— "Culture Memory—China, Between Past and

Future." The event featured five outstanding artists of different traditional Chinese opera genres-including the Beijing Opera, Yueju Opera, Kunju Opera, Chuanju Opera and Qinqiang Opera-who have been commissioned to compose some experimental works that deal with the question of handing down and renewing the traditional art forms. They performed these works in Berlin in March and later returned to meet Chinese audiences. Ten performances-all one-man shows-were staged in five days at two theaters. The performances included both experimental productions and traditional classical segments, so that the audiences could trace the roots of each opera and distinguish the differences between the old and the new.

Premiering in Paris in 2001, *King Lear* is one of the most spectacular productions CLT has staged in recent years. Over two hours, Wu takes on 10 roles, from King Lear to his three daughters, from the blinded Gloucester to his two sons. He skillfully uses props, costumes and different ways of singing to define different characters.

"I portray the characters through symbolic methods," Wu indicates. "For example, a handkerchief, a cloak and the traditional water sleeves of Beijing Opera are adopted to symbolize the three daughters in the same costume."

When it comes to Gloucester and his son Edgar, Wu uses a long stick to separate the two characters: He is the father on one side and turns into the son when he crosses the stick.

"The stick represents lineage," he explains. "To Beijing Opera performers, it is even more meaningful because every one of us must have had the same experience of being hit by a stick during our apprentice time."

Wu adds that he is not only performing the King Lear character, but also himself. "The tragedy of Lear is attributed to his arrogance," he says.

Left: Wu Hsing Kuo in *King Lear*

Traditionally Innovative

Wu Hsing Kuo (left) in *Waiting for Godot*

"I'm also an arrogant person, who will never submit to authority and I'm always proud of what I'm doing."

Wu met the biggest frustration in his artistic life when he created *King Lear*. He adapted, directed and performed the show all on his own.

"I told myself that, just like King Lear, even without a single soldier, I can still continue, I can do it myself," he added. "It sounds quite stirring, doesn't it? As a matter of fact, Lear finally dies, but he does begin to realize what love is."

Being keenly aware of the decline of traditional Chinese opera, Wu founded CLT back in 1986 with a group of young enthusiastic Beijing Opera players in Taiwan, to create a new path for the ancient art form.

Qin - Qingqiang Opera (Li Xiaofeng)

Sighing — Chuanju Opera (Tian Mansha)

The theater is characterized by its adaptations of Western canonic works using elements of Beijing Opera. The artists' performances have successfully subverted the theatergoers' understanding of the Beijing Opera, and initiated a new aesthetic for the theatrical arts. Wu, as artistic director of CLT, has performed the leading roles in all the plays in the theater's repertoire, including *The Kingdom of Desire* and *War and Eternity*, adapted from Shakespeare's *Macbeth* and *Hamlet*, respectively.

Eugenion Barba, artistic director of Denmark's Odin Theater, once said: "Wu Hsing-Kuo shook not only the tradition of Peking Opera but also the understanding of Shakespeare."

"When we performed in the UK, some audiences, who have been watching Shakespeare all their lives, were so excited that they thought Shakespeare was having a renaissance in the East," Wu says.

A Man among Woman — Yueju Opera (Zhao zhigang)

Back in Taiwan, Wu is a well-established Beijing Opera performer. He studied at the Fu-Hsing Chinese Opera School from an early age and specialized in *wu sheng* and *lao sheng*[20]. The versatile artist was also once a leading dancer with the famous Taiwan-based Cloud Gate Dance Theater. Wu has been involved in the big screen, too. He won the 1994 Hong Kong Film Awards as the Best New Actor for his role in *The Temptation of a Monk* with veteran actress, Joan Chen.

However, there are always scholars and audiences who think Wu should get back to the traditional opera form instead of experimenting with Shakespeare or other Western stories.

"They say I am destroying the tradition," Wu says. "But I think I'm tracing back to the traditions. Sometimes our long history is a great treasure to be proud of, but sometimes it is a heavy burden as well.

20 *Wu sheng* are male military figures, while *lao sheng* are middle-aged or old male roles.

Five artists of different traditional opera forms — (from left) — Ke Jun from Kunju Opera, Li Xiaofeng from Qingqiang Opera, Zhao Zhigang from Yueju opera, Tian Masha (lying) of Chuanju Opera and Wu Hsing Kao of Beijing Opera — will stage experimental shows during the "Culture Memory — China, Between Past and Future" event.

"All my life, I've been trying to get rid of the burden. However, after 20 years, I finally realized that innovation, sometimes, is an inheritance of tradition, too," he adds. "Every artist is pursuing a personal style. To me, traditional Chinese opera is my root. I have absorbed the traditions and then exaggerated them to achieve a certain result."

For Wu, the Beijing Opera is the most exquisite among the more than 300 traditional Chinese opera forms, and he has always been trying to make his works good enough to meet the high standards of traditional Beijing Opera.

"Apart from adapting others' works, I have thought of creating an original work of my own," he says. "However, it is difficult to embark on such a project because I always wish to reach the most exquisite level. If I do it, I want to do it the best."

According to him, experimental operas have made some traditional works appear more interesting. Some blurring of facts in the traditional operas make them easier to understand.

"The experimental operas are the flowing water to revitalize the traditional roots. Every age needs a master. For example, the art of Beijing Opera master Mei Lanfang is the cultural legacy of the last century. And now, we're creating this century's legacy together with the audiences," he says.

(Story by Michelle Zhang)

Hablan Mandarina?

Amei Cheung, Elva Hsiao, Dick & Cow Boy ... at one time, their songs prevailed all over the country, but now they are all but forgotten. However, a new group, the Mandarina China Band, is trying to renovate these artists' well-known melodies by introducing a new, exciting element-salsa. The band, made up of both Colombians and Chinese, has eleven musicians and five singers. Four of the singers are Chinese, while one is Colombian.

"In our album, Chinese songs are rearranged in a Latin way," says Alvaro Cardenas, a Colombian saxophonist who serves as the director of the band.

"We also have Latin songs with Chinese lyrics and original Spanish songs sung by Chinese singers," says Cardenas, adding that another three new Spanish songs have been written for the very first album of the Mandarina China Band, *Escucha el Mar.*

Miranda Li, one of the Chinese vocalists, is also a salsa dancer. She has performed in many of Shanghai's bars and five-star hotels, including the Four Seasons Shanghai Hotel's Jazz 37 where Cardenas met her.

Alvaro Cardenas, director of the sino-latin band, is an experienced saxophonist and has produced two albums of his own music.

"I used to work with Miranda in the Four Seasons, she's a very good singer," says Cardenas who had the idea of forming a Sino-Latin band after seeing her sing.

"We started to cooperate in early 2005, but I have been singing salsa songs in Chinese lyrics for a long time," says Li. "In the album, salsa and cha-cha are the main themes."

Zhang Yun, also called Apple, is the other Chinese female vocalist. Though the youngest member of the band, she has plenty of experience. In 2001 she won the first prize of the Chinese Young Singer Contest, and a year later she was the champion of a Shanghai Television Station performance contest. Before meeting Cardenas, Zhang did not sing salsa. "I was introduced to Cardenas for the first time by a Taiwanese agent, and he gave me an audition," she says. Two years later, Cardenas called Zhang and asked her to join his band. Zhang says she likes to sing the songs of Amei Cheung, Shunza, Shakira, and Christina Aguilera. "To improve my singing of these salsa songs, I also

Miranda Li, one of the Chinese vocalists in the Mandarina China Band, is also a dancer.

spent months learning salsa dancing," she says. Zhang is now a complete Latin performer with a hot costume, sultry vocals and fluent salsa steps.

"We must learn to dance salsa as we will be performing in many Latin countries," says Wind Yan, one of the male singers in the band. "I started to sing non-Chinese songs in 2000. Now I can sing 600 to 700 English songs.

"In South America, people all go out dancing at night. Salsa has been their main entertainment. Salsa is not radical but mild and smooth. I think more Chinese should learn it," he adds.

Shirley Maria Carranza is the only Colombian vocalist in the band. She is no stranger to the local nightlife scene, having been singing Latin music in many popular places such as Park 97, Jazz 37 and the JZ Club. Carranza has lived in this Shanghai for four years with her Chinese partner.

Alvaro Ballesteros Cely, president of the Colombia-China Commerce and Integration Chamber in Shanghai, the band's sponsor, says the band will start its world tour immediately after the launch of their album. Their first stop will be Bogota, capital of Colombia.

"Our purpose is to combine both Chinese and Colombian cultures," says Cely. "We are going to promote our joint artistic values. Salsa is the most popular music and dance in our country, and in China it's gaining popularity. It's rhythmic and active and it puts the listener in a good mood."

Cely adds that after the tour of Colombia, the band will play a concert in the United States, before beginning another national tour in China. "We hope to promote salsa and Chinese and Colombian music on the international stage," he concludes.

(Story by Wu Yingying, photos by Shen Kai)

Dancers for a Goddess

"This will become the most famous dance in China." That was what choreographer Zhang Jigang, through sign language, told 21 deaf dancers before they went on stage to perform in front of an estimated audience of one billion people who were watching CCTV's telecast of the Chinese New Year's Eve gala show in February, 2005. He was right. The performance became amazingly popular overnight. It seems that everyone who watched it loved the six-minute dance. The audience voted it as their favorite act in the whole gala.

The dance, called the "The Thousand-Handed Kwanyin" (Kwanyin is the Goddess of Mercy) had the dancers-from the China Disabled Persons' Art Performing Troupe-stand in a long line perpendicular to the audience. This created the fabulous illusion of the dancers appearing as a single person with multiple arms and hands. The dancers stood in a large, arched doorway, enhancing the Buddhist atmosphere. When the deaf dancers performed on stage, sign language teachers stood at the four corners of the stage to remind the dancers of the rhythm of the music, which they, of course, could not hear.

"It's the first time in history that a Chinese dance has been watched and loved by an audience of a billion," says renowned modern dance critic Ou Jianping. "In the past there have not been many impressive original dance works by Chinese performers. Dance seldom catches the

attention of ordinary Chinese audiences and it usually has to play a secondary role accompanying singers.

"However, the lighting, costumes and choreography of this dance were outstanding at the gala show. As a choreographer myself, I'm so happy about their achievement."

In fact, the fascinating dance actually come into being years ago, but had to undergo some fine-tuning before it was presented last Chinese New Year's Eve. "The Thousand-Handed Kwanyin" had only 12 dancers when it premiered in the United States in 2000.

"It was too sparse in my eyes, so I thought of making it with 40 dancers," says Zhang.

The dancers went on to attract more attentions during the closing ceremony of the Athens 2004 Paralympic Games. This new version of the dance had 21 dancers on stage.

"For the Chinese New Year gala show, I highlighted the postures of arms, hands and fingers, pushing them to extremes," says Zhang. "There were not so many postures for the legs. It's a big challenge for dancers, but going to extremes can be the cradle of genius."

Ou adds that the simple gestures of the dance were superb. "Top art is usually the result of keeping it simple," he says.

Zhang's inspiration for the dance came in 1996 as he gazed at sculptures of the Goddess of Mercy in the temples of his hometown in Shanxi Province.

"I was enchanted by the sculptures and thought: 'Why not animate one of the motionless artworks and let it do a lifelike dance'?" Zhang recalls. "It's been my dream for years and it's finally come true."

Ou attributes the success of the dance to many factors, including the excellent choreography, the special skills of the deaf dancers and the influence they and their performance had on the general public during the CCTV telecast.

However, trouble always seems to follow success. Several other dance troupes have reportedly taken over the idea and promoted their versions with pictures taken of the original show. Even a brand of underwear and a weight-loss product have used promotional pictures that are similar to the dance. To stop copycats, the troupe has registered its copyright for the dance. Xue Li, a spokeswoman for the troupe, says would-be imitators must obtain the permission of the troupe and Zhang before going ahead with any performance. The copyright is to protect the rights of the disabled artists, and also prevent the image of the Goddess from being trampled upon.

At the same time, Gao Jinrong, a choreographer at the Gansu Art School in northwestern China, claims she came up with the idea for the dance in the late 1990s, and she is currently planning to take legal action.

"This art form first occurred in a textbook written by Gao, who was inspired by the frescoes of the Thousand-Handed Goddess of Mercy in Dunhuang in northwest China," says Ou.

"But Zhang has altered the image tremendously and raised it to a much higher level. To my mind, both can claim credit for having creatively revived an ancient Chinese art."

Zhang admits that using deaf dancers for this dance was incidental. The idea occurred when he was invited to devise a program for the troupe to perform in the United States.

"I found that they were perfect for the theme and style of the dance," says Zhang. "The legend of the Thousand-Handed Goddess of Mercy is a story of love and devotion which can be seen to be reflected in disabled people's experiences. Moreover, the deaf dancers are incredibly pure and tranquil, making them better suited for the dance than ordinary people."

Perhaps that is why so many people love the dance-the Goddess of Mercy blesses its beautiful performances. She maintains tranquility, calming down the hustle and bustle of contemporary daily life with her thousands of hands.

The Origin of the Thousand-Handed Kwanyin

●An ancient emperor named Miao Zhuang had three daughters. The elderly one loved making herself up all day long, while the second enjoyed only dancing and eating. The emperor's favorite was the youngest, who wore cotton clothes, ate vegetables and loved reading poetry. ●As the emperor got old, he forced the youngest princess to get married so she could inherit his crown. The princess, however, refused to get married and became a runaway bride. She went a temple near the Sea of China and became a nun. ●The emperor later came down with a strange disease which made him feel unbearably itchy. No medicine could cure the poor emperor. One day he heard a voice lingering in the air saying that "Go to the South China Sea to your daughter if you don't want to die." ●The emperor traveled to the South China Sea immediately, and found his daughter sitting in a cave. Seeing her father's condition, she unhesitatingly cut off her arm to make it into medicine for him. Holding the arm, the sad emperor was surprised to see numerous arms beginning to bud out from his daughter's body. In this way, she turned into the Thousand-Handed Goddess of Mercy, who is famous for saving people who have been cast down.

(Story by Michelle Qiao)

Presto-Chango

If it were not for his magic tricks, Qiu Qingzhong, winner of this year's "Golden Wand Award" at the Shanghai Magicians' Club would seem just like your average boy next door. The cards and coins flying between his fingers are like swift, naughty birds. Suddenly they disappear, and then show up again from one of his shirt sleeves. Qiu, better-known as Eric among foreign audiences, speaks humorously with the audience, suggesting that everything is possible.

"On the stage, a magician is the focus [of attention], and is endowed with sparkling witchcraft, but after the performances, he is just an ordinary person, no different from others," says the beaming 24-year-old.

Qiu, after four rounds of competitions in cards, coin, variety and optional magic, distinguished himself among nineteen contestants from Shanghai and neighboring provinces for his all-around abilities. The judges, all famous magicians in China, said Qiu was

Qiu Qingzhong was the Golden Wand Award winner of 2006

Zhou Liangtie (center), director of the Shanghai Magicians' Club, performs with his partners.

good at spicing up the atmosphere and, though an amateur, he had excellent basic skills.

"This is the fourth time we have organized the contest since 1996," says Zhou Liangtie, director of the Shanghai Magicians' Club. "The theme for this year's competition is close-up magic, a popular genre among today's youngsters."

Close-up magic, including card tricks and coin-and-money tricks, is usually performed with the audience sitting very nearby-even at the same table with the magician. This requires a high degree of proficiency in basic skills, such as finger movements and sleight of hand, as there is less room for magicians to hide their secrets.

"The past decade has witnessed a dramatic development in the close-up magicians' techniques, and an expansion in the number and intricacy of their tricks," says Zhou. "Without high requirements to participate in the shows, close-up magic can arouse young people's enthusiasm about this age-old art form."

Qiu, a major in aviation machine maintenance, recently graduated from the Shanghai University of Engineering Science. At university, he developed his abilities in physics, mathematics, science and engineering, and in making models. This last skill is essential for a good magician, who often needs to design and make props on his own.

He still remembers the days his parents took him to Shanghai's famous Great World, where the alluring magic performances opened the boy the door to the magic kingdom. Three years ago, an intern job at a summer magic camp for kids unexpectedly

Magician Qin Qingzhong "plays" with a flower. The 24-year-old won 2006 "Golden Wand Award".

Magician Pan Xuchuan (right) shares magic skills with his American counterpart, Charles Greene.

stirred his passion for learning the art.

"My work was to teach children simple magic during the camp," Qiu recalls. "Trying not to make a fool of myself, I began to learn tricks at magic shops or from watching DVDs. Quickly I was enraptured by the art's charm and mystery."

Today's local magic lovers have many ways to pursue their passion in leisure time, from the Internet and DVDs to the booming magic shops. This is so different from the traditionally strict-but also warm-apprenticeship system in which a student would study under a master.

"The relation between my teacher, Mo Feixian, and I was like a father-son connection," says the 70-something conjurer Hu Rongbin, a student of the Mo-style magic, distinctive for its creative props and stage art.

"He taught us that the secret of becoming a successful magician was nothing else but seeing, thinking and practicing. Sometimes it cost us months and even years to practice and grasp the essence of a trick," he adds.

Though audiences are amazed at the mystery and charisma of magic shows, Hu denies that magicians are supermen with supernatural powers. He stresses that magic is a scientific, visual art, which covers the principles of physics, chemistry, optics, acoustics, mathematics and psychology.

Presto-Chango

"According to the law of conservation of mass, energy cannot be lost or appear out of nothing," Hu says. "But people hardly notice a magician's little maneuver, even the movement of one finger. Sometimes language is also an effective tool to divert the audience's attention and create an illusion."

Unlike many other artists, magicians dabble in a variety of fields, such as program directing, stage design, lighting and creating stage props. Keeping the tricks secret is a fundamental requirement for magic insiders.

Due to its acceptance of varied cultures, Shanghai has always played an important role in China's magic industry. Decades ago, it had famed magicians such as Mo Wuqi and Zhang Huichong, and in recent years it has also brought David Copperfield, the famous US magician, to the city. However, modern Chinese magic suffers from a lack of new talent, funds and marketing, as well as a lack of a more efficient and mature mechanism to promote the magic industry.

"Like Copperfield's performances, we also hope for a mega stage production that perfectly combines traditional flavor with Western elements," says conjurer Hu. "But who would like to invest? In some foreign countries, magic has become a mature and profitable industry ... For us, there is still a long way to go to rejuvenate this art form."

(Story by Xu Wei)

Wushu, for Fitness and Fun

It is hard to find a sport that helps you improve your fitness, strength, flexibility and coordination all at once, and it is even harder to find one that is interesting enough to make discipline sound like fun. Yet, for many learners, the ancient Chinese art of *wushu* accomplishes all of these goals. The name *wushu* comes from the word *wu*, meaning military, and *shu*, meaning art. Therefore, *wushu* literally means martial arts.

Kung fu and *wushu* are essentially the same, but over the past 30 years, *wushu* has been refined to make it more about athleticism, performance and aesthetics, while kung fu remains a combat sport. *Wushu* played an important part in China's history, being used for survival during the country's many wars and upheavals. Today, it is the most popularly practiced martial art in China, and many will attest to its positive health benefits.

Zhang Yi, or Master Zhang as he is referred to by his students, is a one time *wushu* champion. He now teaches classes in both English and Chinese, giving foreigners the chance to experience the sport and learn about the Chinese culture. Enthusiastic and patient, Zhang makes a fine ambassador for the sport. However, his friendly smile and great sense of humor should not be mistaken: This is no lightweight *wushu* master. He will not let up until he is happy with your level of effort.

Technique is everything. The complexity of these highly refined movements is best exemplified watching a class like the one I sat in on. The students ranged from Quan Deming, who has studied for more than 10 years and competed at a national level, to William Richardson, who was attending his first class that night.

Wushu is not for the faint hearted, and even watching can be exhausting. Each routine is carried out at a different pace, as the students take turns to complete the components that make up a performance. From the speed and skill that characterize much of the sport, it becomes apparent that timing and agility are keys to mastering this art. Fitness also plays a vital role and Zhang says people looking for a way to relax and unwind should choose tai chi instead.

"Kung fu is good for the whole body, not just specific parts like going to the gym," says Zhang.

Spins, twirls, cartwheels with no hands and leaps abound, and muscular strength is important. However, even if you are not the most agile or strong individual, you can build your repertoire and exact as much reward as the effort you care to put in.

Zhang himself trained at the Shanghai Institute of Sport, the same place where Yao Ming trained as a basketball player. He spent fourteen years on the Shanghai Wushu Team, after training six to eight hours a day with only one night off a week for six years. His coaching skills quickly become apparent after he offers some handy hints to the newcomers, Richardson and Claire O'Shannessy. They both respond well to his advice, and O'Shannessy appears to be a natural at the art. Boyfriend Archie Hamilton has been here before, but seems to have forgotten most of

The movements *in Wushu* combine to make striking performaces.

People of all ages can benifit from this ancient art.

what he has learnt. Zhang is happy to remind him, and patiently guides him through the moves. Impressively, he remembers his strengths and weaknesses, taking these into account with each tip.

Watching the veteran Quan stride confidently through each action is like watching a ballet dancer, with only slightly less grace and a lot more power. There is something incredibly elegant about the choreography of these performances, but also an undeniably element of militarism in each move.

Dilsad Oney has been attending classes for three years. She had been practicing tai chi elsewhere in China. When she moved to Shanghai, she decided to try kung fu. For her, the sport is about fitness rather than competition, and she enjoys it for its positive health aspects.

Armando Lopez started *wushu* when he was a kid, but he hasn't practiced it religiously since then. Like Oney, he says it is great for keeping him healthy and fit.

One of the best things about Zhang's classes is that they are small. With no more than twelve students per class, Zhang is able to help each student better.

"I don't always remember names, but the body stuff I remember. I know all my students' problems, and you can't do this with 30 people in a class," he says.

(Story by Ayesha de Kretser)

Chime

Chinese Traditional
Works of Art

Fragile Notes

It is 10:30 a.m. Twelve young women dressed in *qipao*[21], with ancient Chinese instruments in their hands and sweet smiles on their faces, form a tableau on the Yuyuan Garden's traditionally decorated stage. Then they start to play.

Several dozen Chinese and foreign tourists happen to be passing by. They stop and listen quietly. They are attracted not only by the euphonious succession of sounds, but also by the strange-looking musical instruments. These are Qinghua porcelain instruments. They are all made of Qinghua porcelain, which is famous for its blue-and-white pattern.

"Our music displays the beauty of Qinghua porcelain, and its birthplace Jingdezhen, in a unique way," says Zhu Liang, leader of the Jinyao Ladies Qinghua Porcelain Band from Jiangxi Province's Jingdezhen City, China's

21 The traditional dress of Chinese women.

porcelain capital. Invited to Shanghai for the first time, the band won loud applause for their excellent performance.

Originating some 2,000 years ago, porcelain in China continuously developed over a period time into various kinds of products-celadon, white porcelain, Qinghua porcelain, and colored porcelain. Qinghua porcelain, which is primarily white with superimposed patterns of delicate, light blue, came into being during the Yuan Dynasty (1271-1368). It

Pipe chime

became a dominant variety in the 15th century. Its patterns never fade. The designs used on it-of plants, animals and other creatures in the Chinese ink-wash painting style-are pleasing to the eye. Jingdezhen, has been famous for its exquisite porcelain since the Southern Song Dynasty (1127-1279), especially the Qinghua porcelain. Its porcelain is praised for being white as gems, clear as mirror, thin as paper, and having the ability to chime. The great fame of its porcelain has grown due to the devotion of generations of its porcelain makers.

"Even today, many households in Jingdezhen open their own porcelain workshops. The centuries-old family craftsmanship is passed down from parents to children," says Zhu, a Jingdezhen native. Zhu's mother was a porcelain maker, and he used to play in her workshop.

"A quiet and small town where tradition sparkles, that's Jingdezhen," say the 40-year-old with a smile. "There, people still lead a simple life.

Ou (a set of plates that can make 48 tones).

Boys learn from their father the skills of burning the clay, and girls learn from their mother how to paint the pieces."

In 1985, the Jingdezhen Song and Dance Ensemble produced a porcelain *ou*, which is a musical set of plates that can make 48 different tones. Over the years, more traditional instruments made of porcelain were developed, including the *bianqin*, *xun*, flutes, chimes, pipe chimes, drums, and *erhu*.[22]

"The porcelain ware, even when shaped into an ordinary bowl or cup, has a clear, soft and resonant sound distinct from any other material," Zhu says. "Besides a device for playing music, each porcelain instrument is, above all, a piece of art. The craftsman creates the body and soul, and the musician makes the soul shine."

Since it was formed in 1997, the Jinyao Ladies Qinghua Porcelain Band has performed in Beijing, Kunming in Yunnan Province, Hong Kong and Macau, as well as overseas in Japan, Sweden, Armenia and Russia.

In 2001, President Jiang Zemin viewed its performance, and he himself learnt to play the porcelain *ou*.

"I've never heard anything like that. It's beautiful," says Michael Murphy from the United States after the 30-minute show in Yuyuan Garden. Traveling around China on his honeymoon, Murphy is deeply impressed with Chinese culture and the rich traditions. "I prefer Chinese traditional music to familiar Western music. I like these performers dressed in folk costumes," he says.

Zheng Wei, a 20-year-old pipe chime player, says she really likes her job because of "its absolute uniqueness." "Last year we performed in Osaka, Japan. We just played on the ground, and the audience sat on their knees.

Fragile Notes

22 The *bianqin* is a set of musical stones. The *xun* is a holed instrument which was prevalent during the Han Dynasty (206 BC-220 AD). The *erhu* is a two-stringed Chinese fiddle.

Flute

They listened very attentively and no one said a word throughout the performance. Then I heard a storm of applause," she recalls. "Winning applause is the best part of being a porcelain instrument player."

Lost craftsmanship

●The history of musical instruments made of chinaware can be traced back to the Han Dynasty (206 BC-220AD) when the porcelain *xun* (ancient holed instrument) was quite popular. ●Later, other kinds of instruments made of various porcelain materials, such as chime, drum, *ou* (musical plates) and flute, appeared and were widely performed. ●In the Ming (1368-1644) and Qing (1644-1911) dynasties, with the Qinghua porcelain prevailing over other varieties, instruments made of this pleasing blue-and-white patterned material also became popular. Some of these instruments were just for entertaining ordinary people, others, if made of very delicate porcelain and with great skills, were performed only for the rituals of the emperor. ●However, the production of porcelain instruments stopped after the fall of the Qing Dynasty and unfortunately, the original craftsmanship skills were lost.

(Story by Fan Meijing, photos by Shen Kai)

China Dolls

For Taiwanese businessman, Leon Wang, it was destiny that brought him to traditional Chinese opera, a brand-new start in his life where art and business perfectly converge. Four years ago, when Wang, a Kunqu Opera fan, opened a factory in Shanghai that produces dolls based on familiar characters, no one could foresee that the route ahead would be tough but rewarding.

"At first I thought it would be an easy job," says the 54-year-old, clad in a white T-shirt and a sporty cap. "But soon I found I was wrong. The number of experienced folk artists in this sector is shrinking. Our work has to start from nothing."

During his trek around Fujian, Jiangsu and Zhejiang Provinces to find and team up with folk artists, Wang discovered that urbanization inevitably has led to a severe drain on talent. Many old craftsmen have passed away, and few of their young apprentices have persevered in this field.

"I have to do something to pass on this glamorous art," says Wang, who has invited several embroidery professionals to his factory and

For Taiwanese businessman Leon Wang, the 500-year-old Kunqu Opera is his lifelong passion. Through the making of these exquisite Kunqu dolls, Wang tries to preserve and pass down the age-old Chinese art.

asked them to hand down their skills to a group of young students from technical schools.

"Excessive pricing competition and a talent drain have made the local craftsmanship industry decline rapidly," Wang explains.

Born into a performing family-his parents are drama and TV performers in Taiwan, Wang developed his sense and taste toward stage art at a young age. His affinity with traditional Chinese opera unexpectedly began during his first visit to Shanghai in 1992. He was amazed by the dazzling show, *The Palace of Eternal Youth*, presented by the Shanghai Kunqu Opera House. The story about Yang Yuhuan and Emperor Xuanzong is one of the most celebrated Kunqu Opera classics.

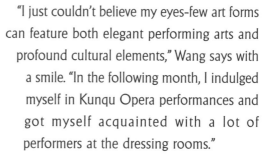

"I just couldn't believe my eyes-few art forms can feature both elegant performing arts and profound cultural elements," Wang says with a smile. "In the following month, I indulged myself in Kunqu Opera performances and got myself acquainted with a lot of performers at the dressing rooms."

Wang started his opera doll business in Shanghai ten years later.

Wang notes that a single handcrafted doll, 12 to 14 inches high, takes the craftsman around three months to make. The production involves more than 100 people and 1,268 separate steps to ensure the brilliance of the creation. In the preparation process, they select

a famous character and design representative postures and opera scenes for him or her. Then a photographer will take 360 degree panoramic images of a performer portraying that character.

"We have invited famous Kunqu Opera performers, such as Wang Zhiquan and Wu Huan, as our models," Wang says. "These dolls strictly adhere to their costumes, properties, postures and even the delicate facial expression."

All the dolls are carved of precious boxwood or yellow cedar. The remarkable facial make-up techniques used in traditional Chinese operas has also been applied to the dolls in order to show the nature and personality of the characters.

"Making a phoenix cap[23] seems to be the most difficult thing," Wang recalls. "All the pearls on the cap are real. Dyed bird feathers have to be added to ensure the genuineness of the 'phoenix.'"

Since the costumes are miniature, it is energy-consuming to do the embroidery of landscapes, flowers and birds on them.

Many opera experts from the Shanghai Kunqu Opera House and the Shanghai Theater Academy appreciate Wang's endeavors in preserving both the traditional opera art and domestic folk craftsmanship.

"Actually, we have the same goal and passion: to rejuvenate our brilliant traditional cultures," says Liu Yuemei, a teacher in opera art at the Shanghai Theater Academy and author of *Facial Make-up of Beijing Opera*. In the past years, Liu and her students have given their generous support to Wang's work.

"My students have gathered much experience through the process of making costumes and props, and doing facial painting," she adds. "Though

23 A luxurious, pearl-studded hat worn by Chinese women in ancient times.

it is tough work due to the long production period, we're still optimistic about its future."

Wang is so proud of his sparklingly detailed dolls that he welcomes people to view their delicate beauty with a magnifying glass. The opera dolls immediately remind people of the splendid Chinese history, culture and art.

"From McDonald's and the NBA to Hollywood blockbusters, we have got used to the rapid spread of American culture," Wang says. "And now we Chinese should also share something with the world. Art can not be confined to an ivory tower. Commercialization is an effective way of raising the public's awareness and preserving our folk art."

To fulfill his vision, his business involves many professionals and young talents who are trying to bring vitality to the age-old folk and opera arts. Wang himself hopes to build a young team who can quickly react to the international market. Making dolls based on historic celebrities and common people, as well as setting up a modern Kunqu Opera troupe, are also included in his future plans.

"Though the Kunqu Opera was included on UNESCO's Intangible Heritage List as an 'Oral Masterpiece' in 2001, many youngsters complain

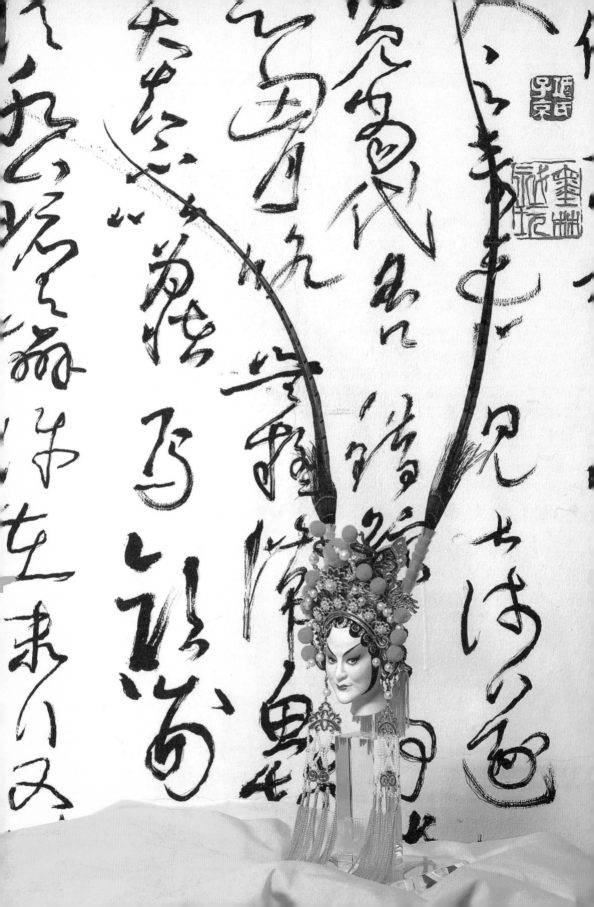

it is slow and boring," says Wang. "It is necessary to introduce changes to create a renaissance."

In his blueprint for the Kunqu Opera troupe, the audience can walk very close to the performers and learn about their vocal and facial make-up skills before the performance starts. After that, there would be a fifteen-minute show including famous martial arts scenes.

"I used to be a snobbish businessman who placed the highest premium on profit, profit and profit," Wang says. "Luckily the charm of traditional opera drew me back to a peaceful mind. It's so amazing. I can't explain that, perhaps it is a direction from God."

The essence of Kunqu Opera

●Kunqu Opera, also called "Kunshan Qiang", is one of China's oldest traditional operas with a history of more than 500 years. It originated in Kunshan, neighboring Jiangsu Province. ●Kunqu features a blend of acting, yet has its own distinctive tunes, which are delicate and elegant. ●There are two main schools of Kunqu Opera-Northern Kunqu, which is popular throughout northern China and Southern Kunqu, prevailing in Jiangsu and Zhejiang provinces. ●Kunqu Opera is not simply dramatic acting and singing. Poetic recital, dancing and martial arts are also included. Unlike Western operas, which focus on vocals, Kunqu actors use elegant dance movements and stylized gestures to accentuate words. ●Kunqu Opera differs from Beijing Opera in many ways. Musically, the *dizi*(flute), is the lead accompaniments for Kunqu, while Beijing Opera features a two-string fiddle called *jinghu*. ●Beijing Opera, which often contains acrobatic maneuvers, is more entertaining and dramatic than Kunqu, which is slow in rhythm and movement.

(Story by Xu Wei, photos by Zhang Suoqing)

Playing with Mud

Standing in front of sculptor Zhang Jianmin's works, it is hard to imagine they are from a self-taught artist who is just "fond of playing with mud", and who attributes his ability to his lack of any formal art education.

Zhang has made, since the late 1970s, a considerable number of works in bronze and resin, including figures from traditional Chinese stories, historical figures, folklore, modern city life, as well as abstract figures.

"Skill is from the unskilled," says Zhang. This is the 66-year-old artist's most frequently used explanation of his two state-level prizes and seven municipal-level prizes.

Zhang became interested in fine art when he was a teenager, wanting to enter an academy of fine arts. However, in his physical check-up before the college entrance exam it was found that he was color blind, and therefore he was not allowed entry any arts academies.

"But my sense of shape was still good," says Zhang. "I didn't want to give it up."

Since sculpture does not highly value color, Zhang started "playing with mud" as a second best choice, making sculptures with whatever sticky clay that was available.

"I found that mud covered rice-wine jars were sticky enough, so I removed their contents and kneaded them into sculptures," he says.

Zhang recalls that he considered it a pity in his early days that he could not go to an art academy, but this lack of formal training meant he retained the mentality of play.

"It has always been a fun game to play, like a toy for a boy," says Zhang, adding that he believes that playing is the most serious and whole-hearted state of a person. "Just take a look at those Internet-cafe-kids playing online games," he continues. "But you have to pick the right career in the first place, then, go and addict yourself to it."

Zhang entered a factory in mid-1960s, working as a locksmith. "I think the work trained my hands," says the sculptor, "which is somehow good for making sculptures."

He has never stopped his pursuit of art, making sculptures with clay and learning, although in secret during the Cultural Revolution (1966-76). "It was because there was no entertainment in that period that I could cool down and learn something," he explains.

Zhang read a lot on Confucianism, as well as the books of Kant, Nietzsche and Sartre, which were forbidden and could have brought him trouble during those years.

"I took advantage of that period to enrich myself, when many people gave up," Zhang recalls.

For an artist, much study and work should be done outside of the art if the artist wants to create great works. "Many artists that I met don't know what existentialism is," says Zhang. "But it is these things that contribute to the most deep-inside spirit of my works."

With the idea that an artist should have a wide breadth of knowledge, Zhang puts diverse elements naturally into his works. He never stereotypes himself by repeating themes: He produces one new series after another.

In his Family Ethic series, Zhang makes sculptures of young, middle-aged, and old couples. This series has been well-received at exhibitions. "It's about a social problem-the growing divorce rate," Zhang explains.

His piece, *Walking While Aging*, contains an elderly couple, cast in bronze. Their faces are blurred and the man's back and shoulder are bent. The woman's obesity is exaggerated. However, they hold hands with each other and are walking together with canes, although very slowly.

His *Where We Once Sat* is made of a common bench, often seen in parks, on which a granny leans against the shoulder of her husband. They both have a smile.

"Everyday we hear stories about middle-aged couples getting tired of each other and divorcing," says Zhang. "But I think a visit to the place, for

example, the bench in the park when they were in love and dated, can be a great help.

"I spent considerable time examining the divorce problem and why couples end up so badly. I think they exaggerate economic problems too much, and refuse to fix the relationship by saying 'our characters don't match each other.' I think a recollection of the young and sweet days from their shared past can stop fighting and help improve the relationship," he says.

Zhang has a number of friends who are senior monks in big temples across China. This inspired his series, The Zen. The series consists of two statues of Da Mo, a legendary Buddhist monk from India who visited

China in ancient times. In one, he is sitting quietly in the Lotus Position. This piece is titled *Zen Can Be Non-Zen*. By contrast, the other piece, *Non-Zen Can Be Zen*, has Da Mo lying on the ground with a finger scratching his itching ear.

"The self-refinery of Buddhism does not lie in the form of exercise," Zhang says. "Not all people sitting in a Lotus Position can reach real Zen-if they are obsessed by desires. Instead, a pure heart, even during subconscious action, can recieve sudden enlightenment and the real Zen. It's like Einstein suddenly finding a solution to Relativity when playing the violin."

Zhang himself received sudden enlightenment when he decided to give up smoking. He went out in a cold, winter night to buy cigarettes, because he could not sleep unless he first smoked. However, suddenly he realized he was enslaved by tobacco.

"Humans must not be enslaved by material things," says Zhang. "To be a man, you have to be the master of yourself, not the slave of things."

Miraculously, his cigarettes tasted bitter after the night, and he gave up smoking within days.

"Buddha will not bless you directly," says Zhang. "The point is, you can handle any trouble if you master the spirit of the doctrine, and the good will be reflected in your works."

(Story by Zhou Tao)

Woven into the Fabric of Society

Dai Mingjiao, 85, began her affinity with the Gu-style embroidery in the 1930s. Though she is now retired due to the decline of her eyesight, her passion for bringing about a renaissance in this unique folk art never fades.

"I wish I could be 10 years younger," says the old woman from Songjiang District with an amiable smile, "then I would pick up the needlework again."

Dai Mingjiao works on a piece in the 1970s.

Long periods of hard work at embroidery has not left Dai tired or even eccentric, instead, it has endowed her with elegance and a captivating bearing that sharply distinguishes her from her peers.

The two Gu-style embroidery works, *Kids in a Courtyard* and *Crane Couple*, on display at Dai's house are eye-catching. Though embroidered, at first sight, they resemble two ancient Chinese ink-wash paintings. Completed just before Dai's retirement from the Songjiang Handicrafts Factory in the early 1990s, the two masterpieces showcase the height of her lifelong art career.

Dai Mingjiao's Gu-style embroidery work.

"Before I do an embroidery, I usually gaze at the pattern to grasp its soul," Dai explains. "Look, in this *Kids in the Courtyard*, the delicate facial expressions of the four kids are the point. But for *Crane Couple*, it is hard to portray the cranes' feathers and the tree branches."

Dai spent more than three months on each of the works. To vividly depict the variations in color, shadow and light, she even split the silk thread into 24 or 48 tenuous strands, making it thinner than a human hair.

Dai Mingjiao's Gu-style embroidery work — kids at courtyard, was finished just before Dai's retirement in the early 1990s.

"Gu-style embroidery absorbs the characteristics of traditional Chinese paintings," Dai says. "It is indirect in message, impressionistic in perception and relatively simple in detail. A successful Gu-style embroidery craft features great dexterity and delicacy, which means you can easily mistake it for a painting at first."

Dai is so versatile that she is not only an embroidery artist but also a painter. She has systematically learned basic skills in sketch, color-mixing and watercolor painting, essential for any newcomer to this field of art.

"The Gu-style embroidery technique is usually applied to ingenious works of art which are based on Chinese paintings," Dai says. "Our needle is like a brush, and colorful silk threads, the ink."

Dai took up Gu-style embroidery when she was only thirteen, a student at the then Sunyun Women's School in Songjiang in Shanghai's southwest.

"In the beginning, I was such a naughty girl that I got tired of sitting for hours," Dai recalls. "However, keeping calm and self-restrained is the point of embroidery art. The basic techniques are not that hard to learn, but to become a professional or an artist in this field, it takes several decades."

Dai's exquisite handicrafts, many of which have been bought by overseas collectors or put on exhibit at local museums, include portraits of the late Princess Diana, the famous Songjiang Square Pagoda, Japanese geisha and Chinese pandas,

Gu-style embroidery originated from the household of an intellectual named Gu Mingshi in the Ming Dynasty (1368-1644). Almost all the female members in his family embroidered. Among them, two women were most skillful at embroidering and gradually developed the unique Gu-style embroidery. After the death of Gu, the living conditions of the family began to deteriorate, so their embroidery crafts were put onto the market. Some official or private embroidery workshops started to learn and pass on the Gu-style embroidery and to cultivate its fame in neighboring areas around Shanghai. By the end of the dynasty, several hundred people were engaged in this craft.

"Many other famous embroidery styles have been influenced by the Gu-style, and this art form has undergone every vicissitude of flourish and decline," says Liu Jianmin, an expert with Songjiang Cultural Center.

Above: Tourists visit the Songjiang Handicrafts Factory, which is known for Gu-style embroidery.

Dai Mingjiao's Gu-style embroidery work.

Dai recalls that she once had about 20 classmates, but due to World War II (1937-45) and the high requirements for Gu-style embroidery artists, few of them persevered in this field.

"Besides, this time and energy-consuming work will not bring big and quick economic returns," Liu adds. "Mechanical production and mass consumption have pushed many family workshops and handicrafts out of the market."

For centuries, the craftsmen have preserved and handed down their skills to the next generation. But now, it is estimated that fewer than twenty people have the Gu-style embroidery skills which would keep alive this age-old folk industry. In the 1970s, Dai enrolled about ten apprentices. Nowadays, they play an active role in passing on this glamorous art. They are also handing down their skills to another group of teenage students from local technical schools.

Though few young people recognize the real value of Gu-style embroidery, its successful application to China's first list of National Intangible Cultural Heritage is good news to Dai and her fellows.

"The list was announced by the Ministry of Culture," says Liu, who also took part in the application process. "Earlier this month, the display of our embroidery crafts at the National Museum of China in Beijing was so successful that thousands of visitors were amazed at the delicacy and elegance of the art form."

Dai is happy to learn that Gu-style embroidery enjoyed a great deal of interest from the central government, and that efforts would be made to ensure that the art form flourishes. "It will have a bright future," she stresses.

According to Shanghai Mass Art Center, exhibitions will be held to improve the public awareness and to find young successors to carry on the folk arts. Cultural elements with official recognition can also receive special conservation and research funds from national and local governments.

"The grandeur of Gu-style embroidery also matches well with the city's signature, Shanghai-style culture that boasts a big acceptance of other cultures," Liu adds. "Preserving the traditional folk arts should be a common task for the whole society."

(Story by Xu Wei, photos by Zhang Suoqing)

Chinese Artists

A Future so Bright

Compared with some emerging Chinese film directors, such as Jia Zhangke and Li Xin, who confronted funding problems when starting their careers, Huang Kai has been very fortunate indeed. The 23-year-old, a new film graduate from Shanghai University, is now shooting his first independent feature film, *Park Shanghai*, with 300,000 yuan from ViewToo Broadband Technology.

"I had the framework for the story early last year," says the young director. "But you know, making a feature is such a costly mission. Also, why should people spend money on a maiden work of an anonymous, young director? So many people have to give up their filmmaking dreams because of a shortage of funds. I can only say that I am very fortunate."

In the eyes of Shi Zhong, the CEO of ViewToo, the sponsorship is rewarding.

"The way Huang is passionate and mature beyond his age has moved us a lot," says Shi. "We plan to post his work on our website."

However, while Huang is the first to receive funds from the company, he is not a first-time director. In his university years, the young man garnered

The story of Huang Kai's "Park Shanghai" kicks off after a KTV gathering and employs familiar elements of Shanghai as its backdrop.

several awards for his digital videos. His avant-garde short films, such as *And I Knew* and *Doctor City*, mirror the living conditions of today's youth in an eerie and creative way. *And I Knew* features homosexuality on the campus, a brave take on the subject. For his new film, Huang focuses on a classmates' gathering, a story familiar to many in the modern society.

"*Park Shanghai* attempts to offer deep insights into the delicate emotions and desires of the city's younger generation," Huang explains. "Different from my former works, the storyline was finally decided after brainstorming with my crew, who shared different episodes of their lives. This makes the story more real and attractive."

The plot begins with a gathering of former classmates at a karaoke bar. Wu Zhengdong, a manager, meets his ex-girlfriend there. She has freshly returned from the UK, and is now pregnant. Since Wu has to leave the city for a business trip the next morning, they only have a few hours together.

"As a native of Shanghai, I have an understanding of the concrete jungle," Huang adds. "The title *Park Shanghai* implies the pure emotions and relations that exist among the city dwellers. In a concrete jungle, you still can find a quiet corner in a quiet park."

A fan of Dayyan Eng's comedy, *Waiting Alone*, Huang says that Eng's movie is a perfect mirror of young people's lives and emotions in Beijing. *Park Shanghai*, with the distinctive characteristics of the city and its people, is *Waiting Alone*'s Shanghai counterpart.

In addition to the karaoke bar, Huang will also use the Jinjiang Amusement Park, and several streets as the backdrops in his movie. Most of the roles are played by university students with no previous acting experience.

"I play the organizer of the gathering in the story," says Dong Wenjun, a student at East China Normal University. "There's always a big gap between dreams and reality. My character in the film is a witness to that."

Hou Wenting, a freshman at East China University of Science and Technology, was selected by accident to play the heroine.

"I accompanied my friend to the casting call, but to my surprise, director Huang thought that the role fitted me very well," she says with a smile.

"I cannot afford professionals," Huang says. "I want my actors to be themselves in the movie, not to perform.

"Without any stereotypes in mind, these first-time actors-many of whom have the same experiences as their roles-only need to express themselves. This makes the film true-to-life."

Huang and the crew have already finished about one-tenth of the shooting. As a directed, Huang encountered a new situation when faced

PARK SHANGHAI

with a scene where characters Da Qing, played by Dong, and classmate Franky, played by Wu Ji, are involved in a discussion. The two rooky actors were particularly nervous about their dialogue. Huang had to spend an hour and a half before shooting began reassuring them that he had faith they would play the scene as he wanted.

"The casual chatting between the two drunken characters burst into hysterical quarrels," Huang says, happy at the

authenticity he managed to create. "They looked back at the past years and the strong emotions buried in their hearts erupted all of a sudden."

China's sixth-generation filmmaker Jia (*Xiao Wu* and *Platform*) was deeply impressed by Huang's passion for film.

"We've had several talks before," Jia says. "He is just that type of young person who is badly needed to bring some vitality to today's Chinese cinema."

Li, director of *Bamboo Shoot* and *Dazzling*, adds that with the popularity of digital video cameras, and people's increasing interest in independent filmmaking, there will be more opportunities for young directors.

"About 15 years ago, I was busy seeking others' support to begin my filmmaking dream, just like Huang," Li recalls. "It was a long and hard road for the film enthusiasts of my generation."

Huang, who is also an editor on the local TV program, *Documentary Editing Room*, says the production of *Park Shanghai* will be finished by September.

"Of course I hope my movie can have a wide release-theaters, DVDs, or Website viewing, whatever," he laughs. "But I know it is not that easy."

Many domestic independent films only have the chance of a public screening at local theaters after they win awards at international film festivals.

"The low-budget comedy, *Waiting Alone*, was the best Chinese film I saw at theaters last year, but it only showed for few days," says Stella Wang, a local movie buff. "Many independent pictures have little money for promotion, but they're really good."

Dr Liu Haibo, in film art at Shanghai University, notes that though a new era of amateur filmmaking is emerging in the city, there is still a long way to go for Chinese indie filmmakers.

"Financing and release are the major problems," Dr Liu adds. "Not many investors support independent pictures unless they have the potential to become excellent works. Plus, these pictures have little chance of being widely seen."

However, there is still good news for the independent filmmakers.

"*Park Shanghai* is just the beginning," says Shi of ViewToo, adding that the company will have a project particularly designed for emerging directors at the upcoming 9th Shanghai International Film Festival.

"We will sponsor more talented young directors and make their dreams come true," says Shi.

(Story by Xu Wei)

Dressed to Impress

If the kimono symbolizes Japan, the *hanbok* characterizes Korea, the sari epitomizes India and the *ao dai* represents Vietnam-then what clothing item represents China?

"*Qipao*," you may say. Or, perhaps for men, the representative clothing is the traditional *changpao duangua* (long robe and short coat). However, there are also the Tang jackets that the international leaders wore during the 2001 Asia-Pacific Economic Cooperation meeting in Shanghai, as well as the Zhongshan suit (with the so-called Mao jacket), which prevailed within Chinese society for decades from early last century until recently.

However, it seems that China's future designers do not agree that these represent modern China. A recent competition, "The National Costume to Me" held by Shanghai Donghua University, attracted candidates from fashion and art schools around the country. To most judges' surprise, none of the students' works were based on the *qipao* or Zhongshan suit.

"We were shocked when we were presented with these young students' ideas," says one of the judges, Professor Bao Mingxin, from the Fashion and Art Design Institute of Donghua University. "Most of the designs were too dramatic or too fancy to be used as real clothing. Very few of them related to the traditional Chinese elements. On the other hand, many showed influences from comics and cartoons."

The first prize went to Tao Yingyan from Suzhou University. Her clothing line, "Calligraphy Spirit", combined the silhouette of traditional Chinese clothing with modern chic elements, such as exaggerated accessories. Tao also added patterns from traditional Chinese paintings to the dresses to create a more Chinese look.

Donghua University's Bian Fei, a student and also a contestant, says the reason why she does not want a *qipao* for the national costume is because "only waitresses wear *qipao* nowadays."

"It has become more like a working uniform or a stage costume, due to the booming development of the tourism business in China in recent years," adds Bian, who won a complimentary prize in the contest.

Qi Pao

According to third-prize winner, Diao Jin from Luxun Academy of Fine Arts in Shenyang, North China's Liaoning Province, the Zhongshan suit was adapted from a Western style of clothing and had no crossovers with the Chinese traditions, so, "it can't represent China."

"We held the competition to learn more about the younger generation's understanding of the term national costume," Bao explains. "Some of their ideas have offered us valuable resources for further study."

Last week, a forum on national costume was organized by Bao and his co-workers at Donghua University during the Donghua Fashion Week, part of the ongoing 2006 Shanghai International Fashion Festival. More than fifty established professors from related fields came to Shanghai to attend the one-day forum.

China has a tradition of changing styles of dresses for different dynasties ever since the Qin Dynasty (221-206 BC). The *qipao* and the *changshan duangua* were only common during the Manchu-dominated

Tang jacket

Qing Dynasty (1644-1911). The *qipao* is based on Manchu clothing that was once exclusively worn by Manchu people. With the establishment of the Qing Dynasty, Chinese people were obliged to adopt the Manchu style of dress. In the 1920s, changes were made to *qipao*, which was then a long, loosely fitted and collarless gown. It was restyled in accordance to a woman's body lines, and soon became the most popular Chinese women's wear at that time, if not today.

According to Professor Li Dangqi from the Academy of Art and Design at Qinghua University, the Zhongshan suit was named after revolutionary pioneer Dr Sun Yat-sen, who founded the Republic of China in 1911 (Dr Yat-sen's family name in *putonghua*, the common dialect of the Chinese language, is Zhongshan). The suit was based on a form of popular Western-style clothing, being an attempt to cater to the modern sensibilities of that time without completely adopting the Western style. It is said that the four pockets of the Zhongshan suit represent the "Four Cardinal Principles" cited in the classic *Book of Changes*. The five buttons down the front were said to represent the five branches of the government cited in the constitution of the Republic of China, and the three buttons on the cuff symbolize Sun's famous "Three Principles of the People."

In an article published in Art Observation, Professor Li points out that it was the people's support, love and esteem for Sun that made this kind of clothing popular. After the establishment of the People's Republic of China, the suit became a symbol of proletarian unity, and was regularly worn by leaders such as Chairman Mao Zedong and Deng Xiaoping on formal occasions. However, the Zhongshan suit was gradually replaced by the Western business suit in the 1990s, and is now almost entirely abandoned by the Chinese younger generation.

"Throughout Chinese history, each dynasty had a thorough clothing system to regulate what people wore on different occasions," Bao says. "However, at the beginning of People's Republic of China, the leaders didn't set up such a system because it was regarded as a symbol of feudalism, which divided people into different levels.

"Moreover, at that time, clothing was not the first concern of the Chinese people, most of whom were still living in poverty," he adds.

Wang Xinyuan, deputy director of Shanghai International Fashion Federation, says that with the rapid development of China in recent years, people are attaching more attention to their wardrobes.

"A country with low status in the international society wouldn't care much whether it had the national costume or not," he says. "However, China, as a country that is playing an increasingly important role in world affairs, is in need of a unique style of clothing to express our culture and identity."

Bao adds, "The 2008 Beijing Olympic Games are coming, the 2010 Shanghai World Expo is coming. We need our own clothes to distinguish us from other Asian people on these formal occasions."

For Professor Li Keyu from the Beijing Institute of Clothing Technology, the national costume does not need to be for daily wear. Instead, it should be formal wear that people wear on important occasions such as weddings, funerals and banquets. Meanwhile, it should also be able to be worn by people from all different levels.

"The national costume must be widely accepted by the people first," she says. "In a multi-ethnic country such as China, the traditional attire for a single ethnic group-such as the Manchu *qipao*-cannot represent the whole nation."

Geum Key-Sook, a South Korean scholar who is currently doing research in China, has been studying the Korean national costume both in the United States and her home country since the 1980s.

"The national costume can be regarded as a nation's symbol," she says. "What we should consider is how to adopt traditional beauty to contemporary fashion design. As with the national flag, a country's special local products, animals and plants, architecture, food and traditional apparels can all be the inspirations for the national costume.

"In countries such as Korea, which are occupied by a single ethnic group, traditional dress is synonymous with the national dress. However, in multi-ethnic nations such as China and the United States, styles of traditional attire are diverse. In my opinion, the traditional dress for the dominant ethnic group in a country should be considered as its national costume," she says.

Recently, a group of young people from different parts of China have established a website, www.haanen.com, to promote the idea of bringing the traditional *han fu* back into fashion.

The *han fu* is, as the name suggests, the ethnic clothing of the Han people, who constitute the major part of China's population. The *han fu* evolved with time as each dynasty in Chinese history, from the Qin (221-206 BC) to the Ming Dynasties (1368-1644), added something new to the traditional clothing style. *Han fu* can be divided into two types-daily wear and formal wear. The former was composed of a short coat, skirts or trousers, while the latter was composed of a coat and a skirt, or sometimes a one-piece dress, characterized by the long cloak and loose sleeves. It is said that both the Japanese kimono and the Korean *hanbok* evolved from the han fu. The han fu was worn by the Han people for more than three millennia, until the Manchu-dominated Qing court came into power in the 17th century, when it was banned.

Many Haanen members make *han fu* themselves and wear them in public areas to promote the costume. Some of them have done thorough research on the Han costume and written papers on various topics regarding *han fu*. Many scholars have also noticed this phenomenon. Professor Bao says that it can be regarded as a sign that Chinese people are longing for their own national costume. He adds that Donghua University is planning to begin research into the *han fu* phenomenon. Both academic scholars and *han fu* promoters will be invited to join in the discussions.

"Although the clothes they make are only from their own understanding of *han fu*, what they are doing, to me, is quite interesting. We would love to communicate with them," he says.

(Story by Michelle Zhang)

Dressed to Impress

Young Artists
Show their Stuff

Ji Zhenhua, like most of his classmates, is busy looking for an internship at local media companies during his summer vacation. The Shanghai University of Engineering Science photography major is due to graduate next year. Now, however, he has become a minor celebrity as his works have been exhibited at epSITE. Early this year, the group of university professors who are regular exhibitors at epSITE hit on the idea of launching a show based solely on the photographic works of students, and so invited students from seven universities to exhibit there.

"In recent years, there have been very few photographic exhibitions focusing on student works in Shanghai," says Lin Lu, a professor at Shanghai Teacher's University. "I remember such exhibitions were very popular among local universities and colleges in the 1980s even though at that time, very few schools had photography as a major.

"Nowadays, many universities have photography majors, but there is less and less cross-school communication. We feel it necessary to hold the exhibition so that students can see the differences and learn from each other."

According to Ji, he and his fellow photographers use the Internet as a

Ji Zhenhua, student of photograph major in Shanghai University of Engineering Science, in front of his exhibit "Children".

medium for communication. They have created a BBS to share and show their latest creations.

"But that's only a small community, and the exhibition will help us present our works to the public," he says. "It is indeed a rare opportunity for all of us."

Ji's exhibit, Children, features a series of black-and-white pictures he took during a trip to the countryside in Anhui Province. With his pictures, he has vividly captured the lifestyle and customs of different groups of children in a small village. He depicts them in their daily lives as they dance, play games, attend classes or simply run around, chasing one another.

"I'm surprised to find the works of my counterparts here," says Zhou Lijuan, a junior student from Shanghai Donghua University who is a regular visitor to epSITE. "Through their works, I see a very similar world to mine, one which I haven't found in previous exhibitions here."

A picture by Ji's fellow student photographer.

If, for students, a photography exhibition is a rare event, a ceramic show may be even rarer.

Qi Fan has just graduated from the China Academy of Fine Arts in Hangzhou, capital of neighboring Zhejiang Province, where he studied ceramic art for four years. Now he works as a tile designer at a Hangzhou-based company. Today, his work is on display at the Pottery Workshop in Shanghai.

Located on Taikang Road, the Pottery Workshop is only a stone's throw away from the well-known Tian Zi Fang, a residence for local artists. Opened in 2002, the Pottery Workshop is the first of its kind in Shanghai, if not in China-a workshop with a gallery for showing handmade ceramics.

The central venue of the gallery is usually used to hold exhibitions for internationally renowned ceramic artists. This is the first time that the workshop has become a "playground" for young students. A total of 19 original works by students from six schools, including Shanghai University's Fine Art College, Jingdezhen Ceramic Institute and China Academy of Fine Arts, are on display.

"China means two things: the country and its clay. For more than 8,000 years, people in

The Pottery Workshop where exhibitions of ceramics by internationally acclaimed artists have been held for the first time becomes a "playground" for student potters.

China have been making objects out of the clay," says Caroline Cheng, director of the workshop. "However, compared with other countries, the ceramic industry is developing very slowly in China today. Chinese pottery has a long and revered tradition but it lacks innovation, and today it seems to be a matter of quantity rather then quality."

"To many Chinese people, pottery works just mean daily utensils-for example, a jug or a bowl," says Qi, who has acquired a thorough understanding of the art of working with clay after four years of study at the professional China Academy of Fine Arts. "That's wrong. Contemporary work in ceramics means more than that-a ceramic work can be a work of art in itself."

Qi Fan's "living", a work glazed yellow-brown to match the color of the earth, features two abstract figures of people — a man and a woman — either face to face, or back to back.

Qi's interest in pottery-making began after he saw the 1990 movie, *Ghost*, which starred Demi Moore as a potter.

"I loved the movie so much that I thought molding ceramics was magic," he recalls. "From then on, being a ceramic artist became my dream."

It is still a dream for the 23-year-old but it is on the verge of coming true. His work at the exhibition, Living, is composed of two pieces. Both feature two abstract figures of people-a man and a woman, he says-either face to face, or back to back. The works have been glazed yellow-brown because that is the color of the earth.

Other exhibits at the Pottery Workshop are of deceptively playful objects which one can scarcely imagine being made of clay. With infinite imagination, the students have made clay into the living shapes of fruits and vegetables, insects, masks, and jewels, as well as bizarre plates, bowls and pots.

"There are two kinds of people who are making ceramics in China-traditional craftsmen and academic people," Cheng says. "The latter group is the country's future hope for the industry.

"Young students here in China study like sponges-they are always eager to learn more. What they lack are not ideas but opportunities. The exhibition is an opportunity and there will be more. Students have a bright future but only if they keep on working hard."

Professor Lin holds a similar view about the photography works by students. "Technique is no longer an obstacle since there are fewer differences in terms of the equipment," he explains. "The main point is their artistic conception. Although students don't have much life experience, they are not held back by tradition. They are always ready to find interesting new angles in the discovery of life."

(Story by Michelle Zhang, photos by Wang Rongjiang)

Shanghai Image

Picturing the Past

As more and more old buildings are disappearing from Shanghai's landscape to make room for glittering skyscrapers, many people are lamenting the loss of some important pieces of history. Fortunately a newly released photo album goes a long way to evoking memories of those times gone by.

Presented by the Shanghai Municipal Housing, Land and Resources Administration Bureau and Shanghai Sanya Culture, Communication and Exhibition Company, the book, *Inheritance*, showcases the beauty of many of the historical buildings that have borne witness to the city's development. From the well-known former office building of the China Disc Factory in

Xuhui District, to what was once the Central Reserve Bank building in Jing'an District, the book features pictures of the fourth batch of buildings listed as Heritage Architecture for Conservation in Shanghai. These feature exquisite designs and various exotic architectural styles, ranging from the Neoclassicism, the French Renaissance and Eclecticism, to traditional Chinese styles.

"The name *Inheritance* means not only carrying forward the Shanghai-style culture, but also demonstrating the elevation of the city's spirit," says Chen Haiwen, the coordinator and photographic director of the album.

It is not the first time that Chen and his group have worked on such a book. They started to record the old buildings with their cameras four years ago, "but previously we mainly focused on the relics of a district, such as Hongkou District, Jing'an District or Huangpu District," he says.

In 2004, they released their book, *Peace & Prosperity*, representing the classical buildings of Jing'an District. It was the first book in Shanghai to provide a full-scale introduction to the old architecture of a district. This experience helped Chen and his fellow photographers to better understand old architecture when they took on the *Inheritance* project.

Above: The exquisite carring of the Shanghai Flashlight Factory on Nanjing Road W. Built in 1910, it's a masonry structure featuring colonnades and combining the Queen Anne style.

It took them three months to complete the album.

"But to present the genuine features of old buildings is never an easy job, especially in such a short time and on such a large scale," Chen adds. "The job became tougher when we were dealing with those buildings that are not in good condition."

Many old buildings are not properly preserved. Either the facade is ruined or the building itself is surrounded by too many other high buildings. "How to artistically interpret the features of such buildings was the main problem that bothered us," says Cui Xinhua, director of the photographic department at Sanya.

How to find a unique shooting angle? When is the best time to photograph? How to represent the architectural details of different styles? Not only did they do thorough research and preparation, but the photographers went to the buildings several times trying to snap the best pictures. "We visited one old house seven times in order to get the best photos possible," says Chen.

All kinds of equipment were used during the photography. "We even rented a four-meter platform and set it up outside the wall of the houses, as some old buildings are best shot from up high," says Cui.

"Another difficulty was selecting the best and the most appropriate pictures from the thousands of photos we took for this 400-page-odd album," says Chen. "We sometimes represent a building in five to six pages, showcasing not only the building as a whole but also the admirable details. However, we also classify similar buildings on two pages, providing the readers with a rhythm, thus avoiding any aesthetic fatigue."

Chen also initiated a photography competition of these historical buildings. Besides the professionals from his company, about 1,500 local

Left: The German-style experts building in the Shanghai Conservatory of Music features roughene for the exterior — walls. **Middle:** The water tower of former Shanghai American School, now a residential building on Hengshan Road. **Right:** The fireplace in Xiao Hong Lou restaurant, formerly the office building of China Record Corporation, on Hengshan Road.

amateur photographers participated in the contest. Some of the winning work is included in the album.

"We just want to show the public the artistry of the buildings through our lenses, instead of focusing on just the historical or the architectural value, in the hope of arousing more people's interest in protecting the city's relics, because without them, Shanghai would lose its charm," says Cui.

To their delight, the condition of a few of the old buildings has improved greatly since they were first photographed three years ago.

"We are planning a series of photo albums to delineate the best old buildings of each district in Shanghai," says Chen. The books will, according to Chen, focus on the relationship between the people and the buildings.

"Buildings are always associated with the residents. People can add a unique cultural flavor to the buildings themselves," he says.

The 400-odd-page photo album, *Inheritance*, is available in local bookstores at 680 yuan.

(Story by Ma Dan)

A view of Shanghai's Bund.

Shanghai the Seductress

She was once a best-selling children's book writer in China, her works winning both the young readers' hearts and critical acclaim. She then switched to literature, writing essays and stories that have also proved successful with grown-ups. Since 1998, she has built a reputation as a Shanghai writer, having published a series of books set in the country's most vibrant and futuristic city. Chen Danyan, always one of China's most popular writers, says her recent years' love affair with Shanghai is rooted in the seductive richness of the city's past and present.

"It is a place worth digging," says Chen, 48, currently a visiting scholar from the Center for Asian and Pacific Studies, University of Iowa. She is carrying out research on the Bund and the city.

Chen writes in her newest book, *Shanghai: China's Bridge to the Future,*

Shanghai has always been a city of aspirations. It has never had the serenity, complacency, and harmony typical of the regions south of the Yangtze River. The ways of Shanghai are a world apart from what was captured by Chinese traditional poetry. Shanghai has aspired to assert itself in the cosmopolitan world. The city was born into an imposed cosmopolitan environment, like a mixed-race child.[24]

With most of its articles excerpted from Chen's four former Shanghai-themed books, *Shanghai: China's Bridge to the Future* takes the readers

24 From Shanghai: China's Bridge to the Future. Translated by Sylvia Yu, Julian Chen and Christopher Malone (Reader's Digest Association in North America, November, 2005).

MISS SHANGHAI

ME NO WORRY—
ME NO CARE !
ME GO MARRY
MILLIONAIRE !

IF HE DIE —
ME NO CRY !
ME GO MARRY
OTHER GUY !!

One of artist Schiff's Shanghai Girl Paintings.

A drawing from writer Chen Danyan — From book "Shanghai: China's Bridge to the future"

on a luxurious photographic tour around Shanghai.

Elegant, illustrative pictures form part of the book, the author's writing the other. Both are of equal importance. Alongside black-and-white file photos recording Shanghai during its earlier heyday, there are vivid, color prints displaying today's city, its people and their lives. Many of the photos are taken by Chen herself.

"Words with pictures is the style I like and I'm familiar with," she says in an e-mail interview. "Instead of weakening one another, the two ways of expression are interdependent and gain greater power bound together."

Indeed, your eyes may first be caught in the brilliant colors of Shanghai, and then, your heart will be enchanted by the city brought alive by Chen's words, which savor the mysterious Eastern aromas, seasoned with strong Western spices of different flavors-over the centuries, the French, the Japanese, the British the Americans and the White Russians have all left their mark.

Chen adopts a documentary style in showing the changes of architecture and the memories of people who have experienced life from back in the olden days till modern times. Her language is delicate, while early traces of her children's literature style-childish naiveté and curiosity-remain.

The book is about more than just the grace and glory of Shanghai.

Besides such famous city names like the Peace Hotel and the financial complexes on the Bund, also portrayed are those dim walkways and haphazardly made mailboxes hidden deep in the narrow lanes of the old residential areas, and the derelict factory premises in the suburbs.

Cafes, jazz bands, Baroque architecture, all things with typical Western characteristics, are also described. Chen writes:

They [the Shanghainese] have a combined Chinese-Western lifestyle that is almost their religion ... in Shanghai, even a plate of salad has been reinvented to reflect the ways of the locals.

"The roads in Shanghai are quite like those in M.C. Escher's paintings, perceived as opening out in seemingly impossible ways and positions. They are filled with circulation and revivals of conflicting

Above: A foreign child in a local garden — From book "Shanghai: China's Bridge to the future"

logic. Outside contradiction leads to their inner order," Chen says.

Accordingly, she pieces together a vivid portrait of an enigmatic city, caught in the paradoxes and promises of the 21st century, with a nostalgia for the past, as well as the East and the West.

In the United States, Chen has lectured in several universities including Harvard, Iowa and Wisconsin, about a book she is currently working on. Set in Shanghai after 1950, it contains about 300,000 words and 300 photos, telling stories about the history, cultures and vicissitudes of the Bund.

"This book, which hasn't been formally named, ponders over the relation between a culture of aggression and a culture of submission, which can not be simplified to pressing and being pressed," Chen says.

"Also it is about how a backward nation walks toward modernization. Nationalism is not the suitable description, involved are men who differ in a thousand ways but who somehow express the same personality."

Though fictional, it is not a novel of traditional concepts, but more a semi-fictional and semi-documentary work, she adds.

The author's story

● Born in Beijing, Chen Danyan moved to Shanghai in 1962 at age 4. She began producing essays and novellas for children soon after graduating from East China Normal University, and she won many awards. ● Her first novel, *"A Girl,"* a story reminiscent of her childhood, has been translated into several versions and received the Austrian National Golden Award for Children's Books and UNESCO's International Gold Prize for Tolerance of Children and Young Adults. ● Chen is prolific with 50 works published. Since 1998, she has written a series of books based on life in Shanghai's past and present, which won her popularity among readers both at home and abroad.

(Story by Fan Meijing)

The Future is Historical

Snapshots of a New China Culture 文化生活

Li Hongzhang (1823-1901) was one of the most important figures in China's international affairs and also a dominant prime minister in the Qing Dynasty. A controversial figure, he was not only known for his proposal to modernize China by using Western industrial and financial knowledge, but is also blamed for signing a series of unequal treaties with Western countries, including the Sino-Japanese Treaty of Shinomoseki in 1895. He would have been more than happy to see a new creative industrial center rising from the venue that he chose for a center of firearms factories. The 2577 Creative Garden might have had no other distinction from Shanghai's booming creative industry without that particular link to history.

For those who are engaged in advertising, design, fashion and art, the dilapidated warehouses, ruins, and abandoned workshops of Shanghai's old industrial districts have become symbols of innovation and imagination. The retro trend and the mania for nostalgia have pushed people to dig out the past in order to produce a creative future. The city government has now opened several special areas for this emerging business sector. The 2577 Creative Garden is but one of the many centers for studios and workshops built in response to this impulse.

Situated near Longhua Temple, a region noted for its deeply-rooted folk customs, the Garden occupies an area of 17,000 square meters. When construction is complete, the whole area will be sectioned into 79 units, varying from offices, cafeteria, restaurants to laundry and galleries.

"We are having difficulties with the renovation work," says Sam Sun, general manager of the Garden. "Some of the warehouses here are categorized as historical buildings, meaning we can't change their appearance."

It is difficult to balance the traditional with the chic, but the 2577 Creative Garden is doing a good job-the cast-steel pillars, the wood roof ceiling, and the cannons are all well kept.

"Today it's rare to have a face-to-face encounter with cannons, except in a war movie or a television series," says Sun. "But the cannons here are real and they have witnessed a lot."

According to Sun, the firearms base of the late Qing Dynasty was later used as the Kuomingtang's garrison command post in Shanghai after 1927. After the founding of the People's Republic of China, it became an industrial area. As planned, the cannons will be dismantled and their different parts scattered around the premises, like modern installation artworks.

Another eye-catching historical installation is a cluster of fire-damaged ruins.

"There was a fire in the factory several years ago," Sun notes, "but we found that some of the ruins that hadn't been cleaned up are very impressive. So we decided to keep them as small pieces of art in the Garden."

Due to official restrictions on the renovation of these historical buildings, most of the units are one or two story. Unlike other creative industrial centers in town, the 2577 Creative Garden is focusing on conjuring up a real garden for the people who come in.

"Each unit has a courtyard both at the front and the back," Sun explains. "There will be lawns and bamboo, because we fully understand what kind of ambience suits people who work in the creative industries."

Nearly 40 percent of the tenant agreements have been signed, according to Sun.

"Xu Zhen, a local young contemporary artist who has just 'peeled off' the top of the Himalayas has showed great interest in the Garden," Sun reveals. 'He is planning an exhibition in a 1,000-square-meter warehouse."

"I heard from my friend about these creative gardens, and I am here to have a look," says Wang Jianwei, owner of a private design house. "The location is very convenient, and I like their concept as well as the whole layout."

In a different section of town, the 72-year-old Spanish-style Derring Apartment will be renovated into another creative center. Located on Sichuan Road near Suzhou Creek, the Derring Apartment (or Delin Apartment) has witnessed the city's massive redevelopment boom over the past two decades, with glass-and-steel skyscrapers springing up and old buildings being pulled down. Nevertheless, the 72-year-old apartment block still stands, and its weather-beaten appearance seems ready to tell an unforgettable story. The apartment is a Spanish-style building with a cloister structure. An old Western-styled building with more than 70 years of history is not rare in Shanghai. However, the Derring Apartment is special, since it has retained its character so perfectly.

"It's the history and culture hidden within the apartment that attracted us to the redevelopment," says Zhao Xiaolin, vice general manager of Derring Creative Zone, which is responsible for the project. "More and

Real cannons with a history of more than 100 years will also be kept. The creative garden was once the firearms base of the late Qing Dynasty (1644-1911).

more people would like to see something special. If they open a shop and set up a studio, they may not want to do it in a skyscraper. They are looking for buildings with a cultural legacy.

"The Derring Apartment charms people with its historic and cultural elements. And it's the first and probably the last old apartment in Shanghai altered into a fashionable creative zone."

The building is like a flash-back to the 1930s, when Shanghai was on the edge of war. The city received bombing for several months, resulting in the destruction of many of the historical sights and much of the splendid architecture within the business areas. At that time, the foreign concessions seemed to be the only places safe from war. Then the Derring Apartment was built. The apartment boasted its safety by showing off its Western architectural style, and attracted lots of upper-class people at the time. Its cloister structure calmed those who had gone through war and lost their homes. Its high-quality building technique employed top-quality concrete produced by the Yi Baocha Factory. Modern Audi elevators were proof of the designers' confidence. The apartment used to host some well-known writers such as Zhang Henshui, Zhang Youruan and Ba Jin.

"In that era, the Derring's special structure provided its owners with a feeling of safety, and independence as well," says Yu Qiduo, whose company, the Sail Consulting Ltd, initiated the current rebuilding project. "We will bend all these cultural elements into the renovation, and preserve some old structural designs evoking nostalgic emotions in those who will be moving in."

The redeveloped apartment, which will come into use in October, 2007, is intended to be a new creative center for Shanghai-a 19,000-square-meter site comprising six floors. It is a lifestyle development that integrates offices, design studios, showrooms, shops, eateries and a leisure area. It is also going to be an active venue for all kinds of exhibitions and events.

"We're aiming at attracting high-end, well-established tenants. Original commerce is what we want," says Yu, adding that they want something special and original. "Distinguished chain stores may not be not welcomed ... as these are boring. [Our] clients will be companies or studios whose work is related to design or art."

The renovation will imbue this old building with new life. The work will include renewing the Spanish-style cornices. Jiong Yan, a 28-year-old Shanghai designer, just back from France, has been invited as the designer to add vitality to the historic building. Breaking from the framework of conventional design, Jiong has done some very creative work.

"We also want to create a romantic atmosphere in the apartments," says Yu. "Bosses may fear such kind of things. But in my opinion, only when you have a romantic working environment will inspiration come easily, especially when doing creative work."

The Derring project has a budget of 270 million to 300 million yuan. "To restore the property and turn it into apartments costs a lot ... What's more, compared with the redevelopment of an industrial site, to renovate an apartment is more difficult and challenging. As a result, the rent will probably be expensive," says Zhao, the vice general manager. "But, the living conditions in the apartment are sure to be better than those that are converted from warehouses."

The Chinese name of the apartment, "Delin" comes from a quotation from the ancient philosopher Confucius: "Noble beings are never alone." Based on that philosophy, Yu says the developers would introduce a space-sharing mode.

"Noble beings are never alone. You can rent an office with your friends who are engaged in different work-you could be a photographer, while your friends could be a designer, a consultant or other professionals," Yu says.

In this way, the tenants can not only share the space but also share services like a receptionist, for example, thereby helping to reduce operating costs. The West-meets-East concept will play a role in the project. "We have found some interesting Eastern concepts. The mixed culture with a creative flavor will highlight the project, which will enhance Shanghai's reputation as a center for creative industries," Yu says.

(Story by Wang Jie, photos by Wang Rongjiang)

Chinese Thought

Zen: The Zenith of Shaolin

In 1987, Shaolin's present abbot, Shi Yongxin, put Shaolin kung fu on the world stage. Through the medium of theater, he wanted to popularize the kind of Zen Buddhism practiced at the Shaolin Temple, an institution founded in 525 AD by the Indian monk, Bodhidharma.

As a result of the abbot's initiative, Shaolin monks have trodden the stages of theaters in more than 60 countries and have made their ancient temple renowned throughout the world. Hundreds of martial arts schools have now sprung up around the temple. The largest one has up to 15,000 students, including many from overseas. However, the actual practice of Zen Buddhism had been neglected both in the previous performances of the monks from Shaolin and in the martial arts schools, leaving people with a stereotype that Shaolin kung fu is merely hard, aggressive fighting.

One show put on by the Shaolin monks, *Shaolin Soul*, a martial-arts-plus-music show, was first performed two years ago. Now, it has been retooled to better present the spirit of Zen and its relation with

kung fu. The new production contains added elements designed to arouse emotions one would feel when viewing ancient Chinese paintings. The performers will demonstrate their martial arts on stage under a waterfall, or on a rock alongside a peaceful spring or in a foggy forest. A gauze screen will act as an abstract temple gate instead of the solid real-life one that was on stage in the original performance. In the new show, a monastery room will consist of an incense burner, a hanging scroll with the Chinese character for Buddha, and artful lighting. The boy monks will sit on five lotus seats, instead of on the ground, to practice Tong Zi Gong[25]. Buddhist music will enhance an already tranquil Zen atmosphere.

"True Shaolin kung fu is a mixture of tranquil Zen Buddhism and superb martial arts," says director He Shuanglin. "I've asked the performers not to wear aggressive expressions when fighting."

He has also taken the advice of Jiao Hongbo, president of the Kung Fu Studio, to sprinkle more Zen elements into this revised theatrical kung fu feast. Jiao says the practice of Zen had been neglected in the previous performances. "With a history of 1,500 years, Shaolin kung fu is rooted in Zen Buddhism," he says. "Shaolin monks meditate, chant Buddhist scripts and practice martial arts every day. But the performances in past years focused only on martial arts, leaving audiences with the superficial understanding that Shaolin kung fu is merely hard, aggressive fighting. Now we want to highlight Zen in the new show which, after all, is the true essence of Shaolin kung fu."

In addition to this show, Jiao's 21 performers have also joined with Taiwan's percussion-based U Theater to create a new show called, *A*

25 A boy virgin's kung fu.

Touch of Zen. The show, with a budget of four million yuan, tells its story through dynamic demonstrations of martial arts and sacred drumming. It was an instant hit in Taipei in 2005, and there are now plans for a 60-show annual world tour. *A Touch of Zen* is only the English title. However, the Chinese title can more literally be translated *Zen, Martial Arts, Not Two*. This title emphasizes the premise that martial arts are incomplete without Zen Buddhism, and vice versa. The storyline of *A Touch of Zen* follows the life of a child abandoned by his mother at Shaolin Temple after a high-ranking general has killed his father. When the boy is eighteen, he learns of his father's murder and his mother's imprisonment, and he vows to avenge the injustice done to his family by killing the general. Throughout the story, both the boy and the general are confronted with the inseparable relationship between Zen Buddhism and martial arts.

To go beyond entertaining audiences with amazing skills in martial arts, the monastery has started the application process to have UNESCO declare Shaolin kung fu as one of the World's Masterpieces of Oral and Intangible Heritage of Humanity. Only two other Chinese art forms, Kunqu Opera and *guqin* (seven-string instrument) music, have received this accolade.

Abbot Shi has repeatedly emphasized the difference between martial arts and Shaolin kung fu. "Shaolin kung fu is a rich, religious Chinese cultural relic, which ranges from martial arts to Zen Buddhism, Shaolin medications, and art," he has said. "In history, the practice of martial arts was used only to protect our temple and Buddhism. Zen is the essence and the source of our ultimate wisdom." That is why the temple applied to UNESCO to have "Shaolin kung fu" and not "Shaolin martial arts" listed as one of the world's cultural masterpieces. With these efforts, he hopes that Zen will no longer be seen as a mysterious element wrapped up inside Shaolin kung fu.

If, through the productions of *Shaolin Soul* and *A Touch of Zen*, the relationship of Zen Buddhism and Shaolin martial arts has finally been demonstrated on stage to audiences, the new production of *Zen Shaolin*, A *Music Ritual* will immerse audiences in the ambience of Zen.

Imagine you are sitting on a Buddhist cattail hassock, with the singing of the monks accompanied by the sounds of water tumbling over rocks, and winds sighing through the trees. This is not a dream from a Chinese legend. A team of artists-including Oscar-winning composer Tan Dun-with a 100-million-yuan budget and a 12-month time frame, is hard at work on an authentic Zen concert that will burst forth in October, 2006.

"I will use rocks as instruments, and flowing water as strings to create natural, environment-friendly music through combining advanced digital technology with ancient Chinese culture," says Tan, who won an Oscar for his score for *Crouching Tiger, Hidden Dragon*.

The concert stage, surrounded by forested mountain peaks, springs and stone bridges, is in a canyon named Daixiangou ("The Ditch of Waiting for the Immortals") at the foot of the Shaolin Temple near Songshan Mountain. An audience of some 2,200 can sit on cattail hassocks in a wooden temple to watch the show. About 1,000 monks will recite Zen scriptures, perform music with stone instruments, and demonstrate Shaolin kung fu. Special lighting will help create striking and breathtaking scenes.

Shi hopes the Temple will be able to rediscover some of the lost Shaolin art of music through the project. "Shaolin Temple has had not only kung fu monks, but also musician monks ever since ancient times," says Shi who has provided Tan with historical material about Shaolin music. "We also have our own instruments and music scores, but they haven't been handed down very well."

If Tan the composer wants to experiment with something completely new, and Shi is anxious to reclaim a lost heritage, producer Mei Shuaiyuan is more interested in the business side of the project.

"Market surveys show that travelers usually spend at most one day at Songshan Mountain, partly because there's no entertainment at night," says Mei. "This show will be an attraction to get them to stay overnight. We have another budget of 250 million yuan to build a Zen Hotel, vegetarian restaurants and a Zen-themed shopping street near the 'stage canyon', In the Zen Hotel, men and women will live separately and attend Zen seminars and classes." The hotel-built to four-star standard-will be a refuge for people who want to cleanse their hearts and minds through pure meditation.

Mei adds that a modified version of *Zen Shaolin, A Music Ritual* will be staged in New York and Hong Kong after the Songshan performances.

"The movie Crouching Tigers, Hidden Dragon implied that kung fu is a kind of calligraphy, while sword art is actually philosophy and beauty," says Tan. "Now I continue this spirit for the Shaolin project. My dream is to make Songshan Mountain an education base for people around the world to learn not only the kung fu of waving swords and spears, but also the beauty of harmony."

About 500 sound speakers will be scattered around the stage, creating a stereophonic sound-effect in the canyon.

"Although there are lots of speakers, the sound will be completely natural," says Englishman David Sheppard, sound-effect designer for the project. "The sound is clear and clean-the water sounds like water. There's no technological problems, because I've been trying this out with Tan for five years."

Tan says that a number of sluice gates will control the speed of the water in the springs to create different, magical sounds. Stones-millions of years old-from Songshan Mountain will be used as percussion instruments.

"Tons and tons of water flow from the top of Songshan Mountain every second, and through technology it can sound like rocks clashing," Tan says. "I've traveled to museums in New York and London, and to villages in Sichuan, Hubei and Hunan Provinces to do research. Now I've invented and refined 15 stone instruments, the biggest of which is 10 meters long. We will make a real rock 'n' roll sound."

With these performances, Abbot Shi hopes the relationship of Zen Buddhism and Shaolin martial arts will finally emerge from its dusty, forgotten corner.

The Key Elements of Shaolin Kung Fu

●**Zen** Shaolin monks seek to bring balance of mind, body and spirit through an intense form of meditation called Zen. Zen meditation calms the body and focuses the mind so that its practitioners are able to endure extraordinary pain, and can engage in the intense daily training required to achieve the high degrees of skill displayed in their martial arts movements. ●**Fist** Fist is based on the movements of animals encountered by Buddhist monks when practicing in forests. Shaolin fists include monkey fist, dragon fist, tiger fist, panther fist, crane fist, snake fist, mantis fist and eagle fist, among others. ●**Gong** Gong-the way to reach utmost strength-is the most amazing and mysterious form of Shaolin kung fu. It is usually demonstrated by breaking wood with one's head or breaking stones with one's foot. There are several types of *gong* in Shaolin kung fu, such as rigid-gong and iron-head-gong. ●**Wu** Wu places more emphasis on technique in weapon skills, and involves great expertise with use of the falchion, spear, sword, stick, halberd, whip, shovel, bola, axe, hook, fork and crutch. The Shaolin staff is the best-known weapon used in this repertoire of skills.

(Story by Michelle Qiao)

Cultural Crusader

Zhang Zhiyi lit a joss stick, took a deep breath and pounded the table with a Chinese wooden fan to commence his class. Attired in an ancient, beige Chinese robe, the 36-year-old taught six children traditional culture every Saturday afternoon this spring, in much the same way that their great-grandparents might have been taught.

The four boys and two girls sit on the ground in front of a tiny antique-style table with an ink-stone for calligraphy lessons. A yellowish portrait of Confucius smiles down at them from the wall. First they recite sentences from the *San Zi Jing* ("The Three Character Classic") and practice writing couplets, a pair of lines of rhymed poetry formerly used to decorate the walls and doors. The wall of the school is graced by the couplets written by these children aged between eight and twelve. There are currently between 25 and 30 children regularly attending the classes.

The school, named Ju Zhai Sishu ("Private School of Aromatic Chrysanthemum"), sits among the narrow streets and bleached houses of Suzhou, Shanghai's neighboring city in Jiangsu Province, famous for its silk embroidery and ancient gardens. The chrysanthemum is one of the four most beloved plants of ancient Chinese literature, along with bamboo, plum blossoms, and orchids. Having a love for the chrysanthemum and traditional culture, Zhang opened the school in October, 2005, with several friends in order to pass down Chinese traditions in a very traditional way. He chose Suzhou because "the city has an ambience of traditional culture."

"My grandfather nurtured my interest in traditional culture. He studied in an old-style private school, and collected piles of ancient books, a lot of which I've read," says Zhang, who used to be a merchant selling decorative materials in Shanghai but has now switched his career to something of real interest.

"The Chinese education system has been influenced by Russian or Western style, and lacks a proper introduction into our own culture. This is what I want to teach my students," adds Zhang, whose table is dotted with calligraphy brushes, a potted landscape, a chinaware tea set and a computer.

"They might only have a slight touch of our rich, deep culture after part-time study here for one year. But at least they won't feel strange or unfamiliar with our culture in the future," he says.

The class for children is priced at 320 yuan for four weekend courses. Zhang also employed professional teachers for adult classes about the tea ceremony, the 《易经》 (*The Book of Changes*) and *guqin* playing, The *guqin* is an ancient Chinese stringed instrument.

The school has been the subject of some controversy since it opened in this quiet corner of Suzhou.

"It shouldn't be bad news that a Chinese opens a school to spread the word of his own culture," Zhang says. "China has been prosperous throughout history mostly, although the last 100 years it lagged behind. Now with the economy booming, we Chinese are regaining faith and confidence in our own culture."

Chen Yinchi, professor of Chinese studies at Fudan University, says Chinese used to believe that their culture was the best in the world in the past, but their faith collapsed after repeated frustrations and Western cultural invasions since 1840.

"Now interest in Chinese culture is reviving as China is booming," says Chen. "In addition to our strong economy, China needs more soft power, like cultural or philosophical contributions to the world, to have real influence. We might find out more about the strength of soft power from our wise ancestors."

Chen says it is good for Zhang's school to offer children a chance to get a real feel for Chinese culture.

"Children will choose what to study based on whether they will be good for them when they grow up." he says. "But our children often know so little about their own country when talking about China with their foreign friends."

Suzhou resident Wang Xin took her 9-year-old daughter to the school because "it offers a good education for girls."

"I want my girl to have an elegant behavior and an understanding of traditional culture, rather than just studying for exams," says Wang. "I'm so glad to see that my daughter's beginning to love calligraphy and has developed an interest in writing couplets. After the class she seems to be more polite to us at home."

Luo Zhou, a PhD researcher on ancient Chinese literature at Fudan University, says it is necessary for Chinese children, who have suffered from a purely examination-oriented education, to learn true wisdom from their ancestors.

"Traditional culture is not all about rules and discipline. There's a heroic, romantic and very beautiful spirit, which will broaden the views of children and shape their good character," Luo says.

"But I cannot agree with Zhang's teaching style, to light incense sticks and wear traditional clothes. It's so weird and unnatural, like a show, and kids will imitate it," Luo adds. "I think they should highlight the active, natural and beautiful parts of our tradition. You can never live a life like the ancient Chinese in modern society. In the olden days they only ate two meals a day!"

Scholar Yao Yuan, from Beijing University studying international relations, says most Oriental countries, like Japan, have tried to find their own cultural identity during their modern development. In China, however,